CHRISTIANITY
IN ASIA AND AMERICA
AFTER A.D. 1500

INSTITUTE OF RELIGIOUS ICONOGRAPHY
STATE UNIVERSITY GRONINGEN

ICONOGRAPHY OF RELIGIONS

EDITED BY

TH. P. VAN BAAREN, L. P. VAN DEN BOSCH, L. LEERTOUWER, F. LEEMHUIS
and H. BUNING (*Secretary*)

SECTION XXIV: CHRISTIANITY

FASCICLE THIRTEEN

LEIDEN
E. J. BRILL
1979

CHRISTIANITY
IN ASIA AND AMERICA

AFTER A.D. 1500

BY

JOHN F. BUTLER

Formerly Professor of Philosophy, Madras Christian College

With 48 Plates

LEIDEN
E. J. BRILL
1979

ISBN   90 04 06040 5

PRINTED IN THE NETHERLANDS

Dedicated to

D.Dr Arno Lehmann, D.D.

formerly missionary in India
Professor in the Martin-Luther-Universität, Halle-Wittenberg
steadfast witness to Christianity
and kindly mentor to all who study its art overseas

The Author's thanks are due to scores of officials and friends around the world, too numerous to name here, who through a quarter of a century have most generously helped his studies by information and pictures, or by courtesies at museums and libraries.

CONTENTS

SELECT BIBLIOGRAPHY

I. GENERAL

Bossche, L. van den, *Les arts en pays de mission* (offprint from *Rythmes du monde*, Bruges, Abbaye de Saint-André, n.d.).

Bürki, Bruno, *La case des chrétiens: Essai de théologie pratique sur le lieu de culte en Afrique* (Yaoundé, C.L.E., 1973).

Burland, C. A., *So sahen sie uns* (Vienna & Munich, Schroll, 1968). *The Exotic White Man* (London, Weidenfeld & Nicolson, 1969).

Butler, J. F., 'Non-European Christian Art and Architecture', in: Cope, Gilbert (ed.): *Christianity and the Visual Arts* (London, Faith Pr., 1964), chap. ix.

——, 'India and the Far East', in: Frere-Cook, G., 1972, 1973, as below, chap. xiii.

——, 'The New Factors in Christian Art outside the West: Developments since 1950', in: *Journal of Ecumenical Studies* (Philadelphia, Pa., Temple Univ.), x, 1 (Winter 1973), pp. 94-120. Also in: *Research Bulletin 1972* of the Inst. for the Study of Worship and Religious Architecture, Birmingham Univ., pp. 16-29.

Charlier, H., *Arts et missions* (offprint from *Rythmes du monde*, Bruges, Abbaye de Saint-André, n.d.).

Costantini, Celso, *L'arte cristiana nelle missioni* (Roma, Tipografia Poliglotta Vaticana, 1940). Fr. trans.: *L'art chrétien dans les missions* (Paris, etc., Desclée de Brouwer, 1949).

Filmstrips (Christian art in India, China, Japan and the Philippines), publ. by the Council of Ecumenical Mission and Relations of the United Presbyterian Church, U.S.A.

Fleming, D. J., *Heritage of Beauty* (New York, Friendship Pr., 1937).

——, *Each with his own Brush* (New York, Friendship Pr., 1938).

——, *Christian Symbolism in a World Community* (New York, Friendship Pr., 1940).

Frere-Cook, Gervis (ed.), *The Decorative Arts of the Christian Church* (London, Cassell, 1972). Amer. ed. as: *Art and Architecture of Christianity* (Cleveland, Ohio, Case Western Reserve Univ. Pr., 1973).

Jobé, Joseph, *Ecce Homo* (London, Macmillan, & New York, Harpers, 1962).

Lach, Donald F., *Asia in the Making of Europe* (Chicago & London, Univ. of Chicago Pr.: I. i, 1965, & ii, 1965, 1971; II. i, 1970; II. ii & iii, 1977. Esp. II. i, *The Visual Arts*.

Latourette, K. S., *A History of the Expansion of Christianity* (London, Eyre & Spottiswoode, 1938/45).

——, *A History of Christianity* (London, Eyre & Spottiswoode, 1954).

Lehmann, (E.) Arno, *Die Kunst der Jungen Kirchen* (Berlin, Evangelische Verlagsanstalt, 1955).

——, *Afroasiatische christliche Kunst* (Berlin, Evangelische Verlagsanstalt, 1966). Amer. ed. as: *Christian Art in Africa and Asia* (St Louis, Mo., & London, Concordia Publ. Ho., 1969).

Luzbetak, Louis J., *The Church and Cultures* (Techny, Ill., Divine Word Publ., 1963).

Neill, Stephen (C.), *A History of Christian Missions* (Harmondsworth, Penguin, 1964).

S.P.G. (now U.S.P.G.), London, *Son of Man* (1939, etc.).

——, *The Life of Christ by an Indian Artist* (A. D. Thomas) (1948, etc.).

——, *The Life of Christ by Chinese Artists* (1943).

——, *In Parables: Illustrations of the Parables of Christ* (1949, etc.).

——, *And Was Made Man* (1956).

Takenaka, Masao, *Christian Art in Asia* (Tokyo, Kyo Bun Kwan, in association with the Christian Conference of Asia, 1975).

Twair, Kassem, 'Die Malereien des Aleppo-Zimmers im Islamischen Museum zu Berlin', in: *Kunst des Orients* (Wiesbaden), V, 1 (1968), pp. 1-42.

II. PERSIA

Anon., *A Chronicle of the Carmelites in Persia* (2 vols) (London, Eyre & Spottiswoode, 1939).

Arnold, Sir Thomas W., *Painting in Islam: A Study of the Place of Pictorial Art in Muslim Culture* (Oxford, Clarendon Pr., 1928; Amer. ed., Dover Publ., 1965).

——, *The Old and New Testaments in Muslim Religious Art* (London, Oxford Univ. Pr., for British Academy, 1932).

BINYON, L.; WILKINSON, J. V. S. & GRAY, B., *Persian Miniature Painting* (London, Oxford Univ. Pr., 1933), pp. 151-163.

BOTTING, DOUGLAS, *Island of the Dragon's Blood* (London, Hodder & Stoughton, 1958).

——, 'The Oxford University Expedition to Socotra', in: *Geographical Journal*, CXXIV (1958), pp. 200-209.

CARSWELL, JOHN, *New Julfa: The Armenian Churches and Other Buildings* (Oxford, Clarendon Pr., 1968).

——, 'East and West: A Study in Aesthetic Contrasts', pt i, in: *aarp*, 2 (Dec. 1972), pp. 71-87.

CHARLESTON, R., 'Glass in Persia in the Safavid Period and Later', in: *aarp* (London), 5 (June 1974), pp. 12-27.

'Christie's' (London), Catalogues of Sales on 5th May 1973, 11th July 1974, 4th Dec. 1975, 13th/14th April, 24th Nov. 1976.

COCKERELL, SYDNEY C., etc., *A Book of Old Testament Illustrations of the Middle of the Thirteenth Century sent by Cardinal Bernard Maciejowski to Shah Abbas the Great, King of Persia, now in the Pierpont Morgan Library at New York* (Cambridge, Univ. Pr., for Roxburghe Club, 1927). Re-issued, with extra pictures, more colour, and changed letter-press, as: *Old Testament Miniatures: A Medieval Picture Book with 283 Paintings from the Creation to the Story of David* (London, Phaidon, 1969).

FALK, S. J., *Qajar Paintings: Persian Oil Paintings of the 18th and 19th Centuries* (London, Faber/Sotheby, 1972).

GRAY, BASIL, *Persian Paintings* (Lausanne & Cleveland, Skira, 1961).

HERBERT, Sir THOMAS, *A Relation of some yeares Travaile, begunne Anno 1626* (London, Stansby & Bloome, 1634; Blome & Bishop, 1638, 1665; Scott, 1677—all with many variants).

IVANOV, A. A.; GREK, T.; & AKIMUSHKIN, O. F., *Albom indiyskikh i persidskikh minatur* XVI-XVIII BB (Mockwa, 1962).

KÜHNEL, E., *Miniaturmalerei im islamische Orient* (Berlin, Cassirer, 1912).

LE STRANGE, G. (ed. & trans.), *Don Juan of Persia. A Shiʿah Catholic 1560-1604* (London, Routledge, 1926).

MACLAGAN, Sir EDWARD (D.), *The Jesuits and the Great Mogul* (London, Burns, Oates & Washbourne, 1932).

MANUCCI, NICCOLAO, *Storia do Mogor, 1635-1708* (ed. & trans. W. Irvine) (London, Murray, for Govt of India, 4 vols, 1906/8).

MARTIN, F. R., *The Miniature Painting and Painters of Persia India and Turkey* (2 vols) (London, Quaritch, 1912).

MARTINOVITCH, NICHOLAS N., 'The Life of Mohammad Paolo Zaman, The Persian Painter of the XVIIth Century', in: *Journal of the American Oriental Society* (New Haven, Yale Univ. Pr.), 45 (1925), pp. 106-109.

MASLENITSYNA, S., *Persian Art in the Collection of the Museum of Oriental Art* (Moscow) (Leningrad, Aurora Art Publ., 1975).

MATOS, LUÍS DE, 'Les relations entre le Portugal et la Perse', in: *Acta Iranica* (Leiden, Brill, for Bibliothèque Pahlavi), 3 (1974), pp. 411-417.

POPE, A. UPHAM (ed.), *A Survey of Persian Art* (6 vols) (London & New York, Oxford Univ. Pr., for Amer. Inst. for Iranian Art & Archaeology, 1938/9), ii, pp. 1365-1390; iii, pp. 1809-1974.

ROBINSON, B. W., *A Descriptive Catalogue of the Persian Paintings in the Bodleian Library* (Oxford, Clarendon Pr., 1958).

——, *Persian Drawings from the 14th through the 19th Century* (New York, 1965).

——, *Persian Miniature Painting from Collections in the British Isles* (London, H.M.S.O. for V. & A., 1967).

——, 'Qajar Painted Enamels', in: R. Pinder-Wilson (ed.): *Paintings from Islamic Lands* (Oxford, Cassirer, 1969).

ROBINSON, B. W.; SIMS, ELEANOR G., and others, *Persian and Mughal Art:* Catalogue of an Exhibition (London, Colnaghi, 1976).

SCARCIA, GIANROBERTO, 'Venezia e la Persia tra Uzun Hasan e Tahmasp (1424-1572)', in: *Acta Iranica* (Leiden, Brill, for Bibliothèque Pahlavi), 3 (1974), pp. 419-438.

(SHARP, R. N.) Anon., *Brief Description of the Church of Saint Simon the Zealot, Shiraz, Iran* (publ. at the church, 1939; also a Persian ed.).

SMITH, VINCENT A., *A History of Fine Art in India and Ceylon* (ed. 1, Bombay, Taraporevala & Oxford, Clarendon Pr., 1911; ed. 2, Bombay, Taraporevala & Oxford, Clarendon Pr., 1930; ed. 3, Bombay, Taraporevala, 1962).

'Sotheby's' (London), Catalogues of Sales on 7th July, 23rd Nov. 1976, 2nd May 1977.
STCHOUKINE, IVAN (S.), *Les peintures des manuscrits de Shah ʿAbbās Ier* (Paris, Geuthner, 1964).
WATERFIELD, ROBIN E., *Christians in Persia* (London, Allen & Unwin, 1973).
WELCH, STUART CARY, *Royal Persian Manuscripts* (London, Thames & Hudson; U.S.A., Braziller, 1976).

III. INDIA

A Arte nas Províncias Portuguesas do Ultramar, Catalogue of an Exhibition at the Museu Nacional de Arte Antiga, Lisboa, 1957.
Apollo (London), xcii, 102 (Aug. 1970).
Apostolic Approach, i & ii (Nagpur, Archbp's Ho., 1956, 1957).
APPASAMY, JAYA, 'Painting on Glass in Southern India', in: *Oriental Art* (Richmond Surrey), xxi, 2 (Summer 1975), pp. 153-157.
ARCHER, MILDRED, *Patna Painting* (London, R. India Soc., 1947).
——, *Indian Architecture and the British* (Feltham, Country Life Books, for R.I.B.A., 1968).
——, *Natural History Drawings in the India Office Library* (London, H.M.S.O., 1969).
——, *British Drawings in the India Office Library* (2 vols) (London, H.M.S.O., 1969).
——, *Company Drawings in the India Office Library* (London, H.M.S.O., 1972).
——, 'An artist engineer—Colonel Robert Smith in India (1805-1830)', in: *The Connoisseur* (London), 179 (720) (Feb. 1972), pp. 78-88.
——, *Indian Popular Painting in the India Office Library* (London, H.M.S.O., 1977).
ARCHER, MILDRED & W. G., *Indian Painting for the British, 1770-1880* (London, etc., Oxford Univ. Pr., 1955).
ARCHER, W. G., *Bazaar Paintings of Calcutta: The Style of Kalighat* (London, H.M.S.O., 1953).
——, *Indian Painting in Bundi and Kotah* (London, H.M.S.O., 1959).
——, *India and Modern Art* (London, Allen & Unwin, 1959).
——, *Kalighat Paintings* (London, H.M.S.O., 1971).
ARNOLD, Sir THOMAS W., 1928, 1965, 1932. As in II.
ARNOLD, Sir THOMAS W., & WILKINSON, J. V. S., *The Library of A. Chester Beatty: A Catalogue of the Indian Miniatures* (3 vols) (London, Emery Walker, 1936).
Art and the East India Trade, Catalogue of an Exhibition at the Victoria and Albert Museum, London, 1970.
'Art India', Pune, Christmas Cards, etc.
AZEVEDO, CARLOS DE, 'Goa, Damão and Dio', in: *The Geographical Magazine* (London), xxvii, 2 (June 1954), pp. 53-67.
——, 'The Churches of Goa', in: *Journal of the Society of Architectural Historians* (Philadelphia), xv. 3 (Oct. 1956), pp. 3-6.
——, *Um Artista Italiano em Goa* (Lisboa, Junta de Investigações do Ultramar, 1956); also in: *Garcia de Orta* (Lisboa), *núm. esp.* (1956), pp. 277-317; also partly reprinted as an appendix to *Arte Cristã* (as below).
——, *Arte Cristã na Índia Portuguesa* (Lisboa, Junta de Investigações do Ultramar, 1959).
——, *A Arte de Goa, Damão e Diu* (Lisboa, Comissão Executiva do V Centenário do Nascimento de Vasco da Gama, 1970).
BARRETT, DOUGLAS, & GRAY, BASIL, *Indian Painting* (Geneva, Skira, 1913, 1978; London, Macmillan 1978).
BEACH, MILO CLEVELAND, 'A European Source for Early Mughal Painting', in: *Oriental Art* (Richmond, Surrey), xxii, 2 (Summer 1976), pp. 180-188.
BERRY-HILL, H. & S., *George Chinnery: 1774-1852: Artist of the China Coast* (Leigh-on-Sea, Lewis, 1963).
——, *Chinnery and China Coast Painting* (Leigh-on-Sea, Lewis, 1970).
Bildmeditationen aus Indien (a series of Jyoti Sahi slides with *Textheft*) (Aachen, Missio, n.d.).
BLUNT, E. A. H., *Christian Tombs and Monuments in the United Provinces* (Allahabad, U.P. Govt Pr., 1911), pp. 27-59.
BUTLER, J. F., 'The Theology of Church Building in India', in: *The Indian Journal of Theology* (Calcutta), v, 2 (Oct. 1956), pp. 1-20.
——, 'Further Thoughts on Church Architecture in India', in: *The Indian Journal of Theology* (Calcutta), viii, 4 (Oct.-Dec. 1959), pp. 135-150.
——, 'India and the Far East', chap. 13 of: Frere-Cook (ed.), 1972, 1973. As in I.
——, 'The Nature, Influence and Use of Christian Art in India', in: *Indian Church History Review* (Calcutta), viii, 1 (June 1974), pp. 41-74. (Largely used in this Section, by kind permission of the Editor.)

CAGIGAL E SILVA, M. M. DE, *A Arte Indo-Portuguesa* (Lisboa, Edição Excelsior, 1966).

CAMPS, ARNULF, *Jerome Xavier S.J. and the Muslims of the Mogul Empire* (Neue Zeitschrift für Missionswissenschaft, Schöneck-Beckenried (now Immensee), 1957).

CHICÓ, MÁRIO T., 'A Escultura Decorativa e a Talha Dourada nas Igrejas da Índia Portuguesa', in: *Belas Artes* (Lisboa), 7 (1954).

——, 'A Igreja do Priorado do Rosário de Velha Goa, a Arte Manuelina e a Arte Guzarate', in *Belas Artes* (Lisboa), 7 (1954).

——, 'A Igreja dos Agostinhos de Goa e Arquitectura da Índia Portuguesa', in: *Garcia de Orta* (Lisboa), ii, 2 (1954), pp. 233-239.

——, 'Gilt Carved-Work Retables of the Churches of Portuguese India', in: *The Connoisseur* (London), cxxxvii (Feb. 1956), pp. 35-39.

——, 'Algumas Observações acerca de Arquitectura da Companhia de Jesus no Distrito de Goa', in: *Garcia de Orta* (Lisboa), núm. esp. (1956), pp. 257-272.

——, 'Igrejas de Goa', in: *Garcia de Orta* (Lisboa), núm. esp. (1956), pp. 331-336.

Christian Art in India (Lucknow, Commission on Christian Literature, Methodist Church in Southern Asia, 1958) (in Engl. and Hindi).

CLARKE, BASIL F. L., *Anglican Cathedrals outside the British Isles* (London, S.P.C.K., 1958), chap. i (pp. 10-24).

CLARKE, C. STANLEY, *Indian Drawings: Thirty Mogul Paintings of the School of Jahāngīr in the Wantage Collection* (London, H.M.S.O., 1922).

COOMARASWAMY, ANANDA KARL: *Rajput Painting* (London, Oxford Univ. Pr., 1946; Delhi, etc., Motilal Banarsidass, 1977).

COSTANTINI, CELSO, As in I; 1949: II, iv (pp. 270-292).

COUSENS, HENRY, *Bījāpūr and its Architectural Remains* (Bombay, Govt Central Pr., 1916).

COUTO, JOÃO, *Alguns Subsidios para o Estudo Técnico das Peças de Ourivesaria no Estilo denominado Indo-Português: Tres Peças de Prata que pertenceram ao Convento do Carmo do Vidigueira* (Lisboa, 1928).

——, 'A Prataria Indo-Portuguesa—Elementos Decorativos', in *Garcia de Orta* (Lisboa), núm. esp. (1956), pp. 273-276.

CRAVEN, ROY C., *A Concise History of Indian Art* (London, Thames & Hudson, 1976), pp. 202-244.

DEVAPRIAM, EMMA, Typescript of Ph.D. Thesis on Mughal Christian Paintings, at Case Western Reserve Univ., Cleveland, Ohio.

EDMOND, FR., *Gospel Scenes in Indian Dance* (Allahabad, C.C.H.M., 1955) (in Engl. and Hindi).

EDWARDS, RALPH, & CODRINGTON, K. DE B., 'The Indian Period of European Furniture', in: *Apollo* (London), xxi (1935), pp. 67-71, 130-134, 187-192, 335-338; xxii (1935), pp. 13-18.

ETTINGHAUSEN, RICHARD, *Paintings of the Sultans and Emperors of India* (Delhi, 1961).

——, 'New Pictorial Evidence of Catholic Missionary Activity in Mughal India (Early XVIIth Century)', in: Rahner, Hugo, & Severus, E. von (eds): *Perennitas* (Münster, Aschendorff, 1963), pp. 385-396.

FALK, TOBY SMART, ELLEN S. & SKELTON, ROBERT, *Indian Painting, Mughal and Rajput, and a Sultanate Manuscript:* Catalogue of an Exhibition (London, Colnaghi, 1978).

FERRÃO, BERNARDO, *Imaginaria de Marfim Luso-Oriental no Collecções do Porto; sep. do vol.: O Porto e os Descobrimentos* (Porto, 1972).

FIGREDO, B. A., *Bones of St. Thomas and the Antique Casket at Mylapore, Madras* (Madras, Christian Lit. Soc., 1972).

Film, *The Lotus and the Cross:* with dance-sequences of the Crucifixion and the Resurrection; produced in 1973 by Gateway Film Productions (London & Bristol), for the Church of South India and a group of associated British Churches.

FONSECA, J. NICOLAUDA, *An Historical and Archaeological Sketch of the City of Goa* (Bombay, Thacker, 1875).

FOSTER, [Sir] WILLIAM (ed.), *The Embassy of Sir Thomas Roe to the Court of the Great Mogul, 1615-1619* (London, Hakluyt Soc., 1899; reprinted Nendeln, Liechtenstein, Kraus Reprint Ltd., 1967).

——, 'British Artists in India, 1760-1820', in Walpole Soc., xix (1930-1).

GASCOIGNE, BAMBER, *The Great Moghuls* (London, Cape, 1971), pp. 110-116, 149-154, 160, 182, 199-201, 229, 247-248.

George Chinnery, 1774-1852, Catalogue of an Exhibition (London, Arts Council, 1957).

GOETZ, H., *India: Five Thousand Years of Indian Art* (London, Methuen, 1959, 1964), chaps vi, vii (pp. 197-250).

GRAY, BASIL, *Rajput Painting* (London, Faber, 1948).

GUNE, V. T., *Ancient Shrines of Goa* (Panjim, Govt Dept of Information, 1965).

——, *Churches of Goa* (Panjim, Govt Dept of Information, 1965).
HARGREAVES, CECIL, *25 Indian Churches* (Delhi, I.S.P.C.K., for Bishop's College, Calcutta, 1975).
HARRISON, J. B., 'The Portuguese', in: Basham, A. L. (ed.): *A Cultural History of India* (Oxford, Clarendon Pr., 1975), pp. 337-347.
HOSTEN, H., *Antiquities from San Thomé and Mylapore* (Mylapore, Diocese, 1936).
——, 'European Art at the Moghul Court', in: *Journal of the United Provinces Historical Society* (Calcutta), ii, 2 (1922).
Indian Culture and the Fulness of Christ (Madras, Catholic Centre, 1957).
IRWIN, JOHN, 'Reflections on Indo-Portuguese Art', in: *Burlington Magazine*, (London) xcvii.633 (Dec. 1955), pp. 386-390.
JAMES, JOSEF (ed.), *Indian Art since the Early 40's* (Madras, Artists' Handicrafts Assoc. of Cholamandel, 1974).
JENNES, J., *Invloed der Vlaamsche Prentkunst in Indië, China en Japan tijdens de XVI en XVII eeuw* (Leuven, Davidsfonds, 1947).
——, 'De Uitstraling van de Vlaamse Prentkunst in Indië, China en Japan tijdens de XVIe en XVIIe eeuw: Enkele nieuwe gegevens', in: *Miscellanea Jozef Duverger* (Gent, 1968).
JYOTI SAHI, *Und das Wort ist Fleisch geworden* (Nürnberg, Missions-Prokur S.J., 1976). Engl. ed., Pune, Art India.
KÜHNEL, E., & GOETZ, H., *Indische Buchmalereien aus dem Jahângîr-Album der Staatsbibliothek zu Berlin* (Berlin, Scarabaeus Verlag, 1924). Engl. ed. as: *Indian Book Painting from Jahāngir's Album in the State Library in Berlin* (London, Kegan Paul, 1926).
LEDERLE, MATTHEW R., 'Art India: Christian Paintings in Indian Style: Experience of a Publisher', in: *Jeevahara: A Journal of Christian Interpretation*, ii. 9 (May/June 1972), pp. 274-284.
——, 'Interpreting Christ through Indian Art', in: *The Indian Journal of Theology* (Calcutta), xiii, 3/4 (July/Dec. 1974), pp. 232-241.
LEHMANN, (E.) ARNO, As in I.
[LOPES, ANTÓNIO DOS MÁRTIRES], *Vehla-Goa: Guia histórico* (Goa, Imprensa Nacional, 1952).
LÖWENSTEIN, FELIX ZU, *Christliche Bilder in altindischer Malerei* (Münster, Aschendorff, 1958).
LUZBETAK, Louis J., As in I.
MACLAGAN, Sir EDWARD (D.), As in II.
MALENFANT, Mgr JÉRÔME, *L'adaptation des arts liturgiques en Inde* (offprint from: *Rythmes du monde*, Bruges, Abbaye de Saint-André), v, 3/4 (1957)).
MANUCCI, NICCOLAO, As in II.
MAZUMDAR, NIRODE, *Drawings by Fourteen Contemporary Artists of Bengal* (Calcutta, Kala Mandir, 1970).
Missionskalender 1975 (Aachen, Missio).
MITTERWALLNER, GRITLI VON, *Chaul: Eine unerforschte Stadt an der Westküste Indiens* (Berlin, Walter de Gruyter, 1964). Engl. ed. in preparation.
MULLINS, EDWARD, *F. N. Souza* (London, Blond, 1962).
NILSSON, STEN, *European Architecture in India, 1750-1850* (London, Faber, 1968).
NORBERT, FR., *Mémoires historiques* (vols I & II, 3rd ed., Besançon, Le Fevre, 1747; vol. III, Londres, Les Libraires Francois, 1751).
O Oriente Português (Nova Goa, later Bastorá, 1904 on).
PAYNE, C. H., *Akbar and the Jesuits* (trans. and ed. of Du Jarric: *Histoire* (1608/14)) (London, Routledge, 1926).
PEREIRA, JOSÉ, Various articles in: *Sunday Navhind Times* (Panjim), 28th June, 22nd July, 23rd Aug., 18th Oct., 1970; 22nd July, 1973; *Goa Today*, June, July, Aug., Sept., 1970; *The Times Weekly* (Bombay), 6th Sept. and 4th Nov., 1973. To be collected in: *Goan Shrines and Manors* (Mulk Raj Anand).
Portugal na Índia, na China e no Japão, Catalogue of an Exhibition at the Museu Nacional de Arte Antiga, Lisboa, 1954.
PRASAD, RAM CHANDRA, *Early English Travellers in India* (Delhi, etc., Motilal Banarsi Dass, 1965).
RAWLINSON, H. G., *British Beginnings in Western India, 1579-1657* (Oxford, Clarendon Pr., 1920), pp. 134-138.
REYNOLDS, GRAHAM, 'British Artists in India', in: *The Art of India and Pakistan* (London, 1950), pp. 183-191.
SCHURHAMMER, GEORG, *Der Silberschrein des Hl. Franz Xaver in Goa* (reprint from *Münster* (München), vii, 5/6 (May/June 1954)).
SLOMANN, VILHELM, 'Elfenbeinreliefs auf zwei singhalesischen Schreinen des 16. Jahrhunderts', in: *Pantheon* (Munich), 10.12 (Dec. 1937), pp. 357-364, and 11.1 (Jan. 1938), pp. 12-22.

SMITH, VINCENT A., As in II.

SNEAD, STELLA, *Ruins in Jungles* (London, Hamish Hamilton, 1962), chap. 'Bassein'.

S.P.G. (now U.S.P.G.), First two items as in I.

STCHOUKINE, IVAN, *La peinture indienne à l'epoque des Grands Moghols* (Paris, Leroux, 1929).

TAKENAKA, MASAO, *Christian Art in Asia* (Tokyo, Kyo Bun Kwan, in association with the Christian Conference of Asia, 1975).

TAYLOR, RICHARD W., *Jesus in Indian Paintings* (Madras, Christian Lit. Soc., for C.I.S.R.S., 1975).

THOMAS, P., *Churches of India* (New Delhi, Govt Pr., 1964).

WELCH, STUART [CARY], *The Art of Mughal India*: Catalogue of an Exhibition (New York, Asia Soc., 1968).

——, *Imperial Mughal Painting* (London, Chatto & Windus, 1978).

——, *Room for Wonder: Indian Painting during the British Period, 1760-1880*: Catalogue of an Exhibition (New York, American Federation of Arts, 1978).

WELLESZ, EMMY, *Akbar's Religious Thought reflected in Mogul Painting* (London, Allen & Unwin, 1952).

WILKINSON, J. V. S., *Mughal Painting* (London, Faber, 1948).

IV. SOUTH-EAST ASIA

BLAND, ROBERT NORMAN, *Historical Tombstones of Malacca—mostly of Portuguese Origin* (London, Elliot Stock, 1905).

COSTANTINI, CELSO, As in I.

FLEMING, D. J., As in I.

FRANÇA, ANTONIO PINTO DA, *Portuguese Influence in Indonesia* (Djakarta, Gunung Agung, 1970).

HOFMANN, RUEDI, & PRIER, KARL-EDMUND, *Neue Kunst aus Indonesien* (Puskat, 1971).

HOLT, CLAIRE: *Art in Indonesia: Continuities and Change* (Ithaca, N.Y., Cornell Univ. Pr., 1967).

LEHMANN, (E.) ARNO, As in I.

LUZBETAK, LOUIS J., As in I.

MYLIUS, Dr., 'Wayang Sulah und Waygang Wahju, zwei moderne Waygang-Arten Javas', in: *Archiv für Völkerkunde* (Wien), xvi (1961).

OLICHON, Mgr ARMAND, *Le Père Six* (Paris, Bloud & Gay). Engl. trans. as: *Father Six* (London, Burns & Oates, 1954).

V. CHINA

Actes du Colloque International de Sinologie: La Mission Française de Pékin aux XVIIe et XVIIIe siècles, Centre de Recherches Interdisciplaire de Chantilly (CERIC), 20-22 sept. 1974 (Paris, Les Belles Lettres, 1976).

ADAM, MAURICE, *Yuen Ming Yuen: L'œuvre architecturale des Jésuites anciens au XVIIIe siècle* (Peiping, 1936).

ATTIRET, FR., Letter of 1st Nov. 1749 in: *Lettres édifiantes et curieuses*, xxvii (Paris, Guerin, 1794), pp. 1-61.

BERNARD, HENRI, *Aux origines du cimitière de Chala: Le don princier de la Chine au Père Ricci (1610-1611)* (Tientsin, Mission de Sienshien, 1934).

——, 'L'art chrétien en Chine au temps du Père Matthieu Ricci', in: *Revue d'histoire des missions* (Paris), 12 (1935), pp. 129-229.

——, *Le Frère Attiret au service de K'ien-lung (1739-1768): Sa première biographie écrite par le P. Amiot, réédité avec notes explicatives et commentaires historiques* (Shanghai, Univ. Aurore, 1943).

BEURDELEY, CECILE & MICHEL, *Guiseppe Castiglione: A Jesuit Painter at the Court of the Chinese Emperors* (Rutland, Vt & Tokyo, Tuttle, 1971).

——, *Guide du connaisseur de la céramique chinoise* (Fribourg, Office du Livre, 1974). Engl. ed. as: *Chinese Ceramics* (London, Thames & Hudson, 1974). Pp. 264-268 of Engl. ed.

BEURDELEY, MICHEL, *Porcelaine de la Compagnie des Indes* (Fribourg, Sw., Office du Livre, 1962). Engl. trans. as: *Porcelain of the East India Companies* (London, Barrie & Rockliff, 1962).

BORNEMANN, FRITZ, *Ars Sacra Pekinensis* (Germ. text) (Mödling bei Wien, Missionsdruckerei St Gabriel, 1950).

BOXER, C. R., *Macau na Época da Restauração: Macau Three Hundred Years Ago* (Macau, Imprensa Nacional, 1942).

——, *Fidalgos in the Far East: 1550-1770* (The Hague, Nijhoff, 1936; 2nd rev. ed., 1948; 3rd rev. ed., Hong Kong, etc., Oxford Univ. Pr., 1968).

——, *The Great Ship from Amacon: Annals of Macao and the Old Japan Trade, 1555-1640* (Lisboa, Centro de Estudos Históricos Ultramarinos, 1959).

BUTLER, J. F., In Frere-Cook, Gervis (ed.), as in I; chap. 13.

COSTANTINI, CELSO, As in I, 1949; II, i (pp. 205-232).

CRONIN, VINCENT, *The Wise Man from the West* (London, Hart-Davis, 1955; Collins, Fontana ed., 1961).

CUMMINS, J. S. (ed.), *The Travels and Controversies of Friar Domingo Navarrete, 1618-1686* (2 vols) (Cambridge, Univ. Pr., for Hakluyt Soc., 1962).

DEHERGNE, JOSEPH, *Repertoire des Jésuites de Chine de 1552 a 1800* (Roma, Inst. Hist. S.I., & Paris, Letouzey & Ané, 1973).

DUNNE, GEORGE H., *Generation of Giants* (London, Burns & Oates, & Notre Dame, Ind., Univ. Pr., 1962). Fr. trans. as: *Chinois avec les Chinois* (Paris, Centurion, 1964).

ELIA, PASQUALE D', *Le origini dell'arte cristiana cinese* (Roma, Reale Accademia d'Itália, 1939).

——, *Fonti Ricciane* (Roma, Libreria dello Stato, 1942/9).

FERRÃO DE TAVARES E TÁVORA, BERNARDO, *Un Triptico Seicentista Sino-Português de Marfim* (Guimarães, 1972; sep. do: *Revista Gil Vicente*, xxiii, 5 & 6).

FRANKE, WOLFGANG, *China and the West* (Oxford, Blackwell, 1967), pp. 34-65. Earlier Germ. ed. as: *China und das Abendland* (Göttingen, Vandenhoeck & Ruprecht).

GALLAGHER, LOUIS J., *China in the Sixteenth Century: The Journals of Matthew Ricci, 1583-1610* (New York, Random Ho., 1953).

HOWARD, DAVID, AYRES, JOHN, *China for the West: Chinese Porcelain and other Decorative Arts for Export illustrated from the Mottahedeh Collection* (2 vols) (London, Philip Watson Publishers, 1978).

HUGO-BRUNT, M., 'An Architectural Survey of the Jesuit Seminary Church of St. Paul's, Macao', in: *Journal of Oriental Studies* (Hong Kong Univ.), I, ii (1953), pp. 327-344.

——, 'The Jesuit Seminary and Church of St. Joseph, Macao', in: *Journal of the Society for Architectural Historians* (Philadelphia), xv, 3 (Oct. 1956), pp. 24-30.

——, 'The Convent and Church of St Dominic at Macao', in: *Journal of Oriental Studies* (Hong Kong Univ.), iv, 1/2 (1957), pp. 66-75; and note by J. M. Braga, pp. 76-78.

——, 'The Church and Former Monastery of St. Augustine, Macao', in: *Journal of the Society of Architectural Historians* (Philadelphia), xix, 2 (May 1960), pp. 69-75.

HYDE, J. A. LLOYD, ESPIRITO SANTO, RICARDO P. & MALTA, EDUARDO, *Chinese Porcelain for the European Market*. (Lisbon 1956)

JOURDAIN, MARGARET, & JENYNS, R. SOAME, *Chinese Export Art in the Eigteenth Century* (Feltham, Country Life, 1950; Spring Books, 1967).

LANCASTER, Clay, 'The "European Palaces" of Yüan Ming Yüan', in: *Gazette des Beaux Arts* (Paris), vi sér., xxxiv, No. 982 (Oct. 1961), pp. 262-287.

LE CORBEILLER, CLAIRE, *China Trade Porcelain*.

LEHMANN, (E.) ARNO, As in I.

LOEHR, GEORGE, 'Missionary-Artists at the Manchu Court', in: *Transactions of the Oriental Ceramic Society* (London), 34 (1962/3, publ. 1964), pp. 51-67.

——, 'European Artists at the Chinese Court', in: Watson, W. (ed.): *The Westward Influence of the Chinese Arts* (London, Univ., Percival David Found., 1972), pp. 33-42.

LUNSINGH SCHEURLEER, D. F., *Chinese Export Porcelain: Chine de Commande* (London, Faber, 1974). Dutch ed., Hilversum, de Haan, 1966.

McCALL, JOHN E., 'Early Jesuit Art in the Far East', in: *Artibus Asiae* (Ascona, Sw.), xi, 1/2 (1948), pp. 45-69.

MONTALTO DE JESUS, C. A., *Historic Macao* (Hong Kong, Kelly & Walsh, 1902; 2nd ed., Macao, Salesian Pr., 1926).

PENKALA, MARIA, *Far Eastern Ceramics: Marks and Decorations* (The Hague, Mouton, 1963).

PHILLIPS, JOHN GOLDSMITH, *China-Trade Porcelain* (Cambridge, Mass., Harvard Univ. Pr., 1956).

PICARD, RENÉ, *Les peintres jésuites à la cour de Chine* (Grenoble, Ed. des 4 Seigneurs, 1973).

PLANCHET, J.-M., *Le cimetière et les œuvres catholiques de Chala, 1610-1923* (Pékin, 1928).

PRANDI, F., *Memoires of Father Ripa during Thirteen Years' Residence at the Court of Peking* (London, Murray, 1844).

ROWBOTHAM, A. H., *Missionary and Mandarin* (Berkeley, Univ. of California Pr., 1942).

SCHÜLLER, SEPP, 'P. M. Ricci und die christliche Kunst', in: *Die katholischen Missionen* (Düsseldorf), lxiv (1936), pp. 3-8.

——, *Die Geschichte der christlichen Kunst in China* (Berlin, Klinkhardt & Biermann, 1940).

SHEK-KAI-NUNG, & SKINSNES, OLAF K., *Sketches of Christ from a Chinese Brush* (Minneapolis, Augsburg Publ. Ho., 1956).

SICKMAN, LAWRENCE, & SOPER, ALEXANDER, *The Art and Architecture of China* (Harmondsworth, Penguin, 1956, rev. ed. 1960, 1968), p. 189.

SILVA REGO, ANTÓNIO DA, *A Presença da Portugal em Macau* (Lisboa, Agência Geral das Colónias, 1946).

SIRÉN, OSVALD, *The Imperial Palaces of Peking* (Fr. & Engl.) (Paris & Brussels, G. van Oest; reprint New York, AMS Pr., 1975).

S.P.G. (now U.S.P.G.), As in I, third and fourth items.

SULLIVAN, MICHAEL, *A Short History of Chinese Art* (London, Faber, 1967); rev. ed. as: *The Arts of China* (London, Thames & Hudson, 1973), pp. 212-217, 225-228, in 1973 ed.

——, *The Meeting of Eastern and Western Art* (London, Thames & Hudson, 1973), chaps 2, 3, 5.

SULLIVAN, MICHAEL, & CAHILL, JAMES, Lectures, in: *Proceedings of the International Symposium on Chinese Painting* (1970) (Taipei, Taiwan, National Palace Museum, 1972), pp. 593-720.

WANG, C. C. (ed.), *The Gospel in Chinese Art* (Hong Kong, Christian Mission to Buddhists, Tao Fong Shan, 1964).

VI. JAPAN

BARETTO, MANUEL: *Cruz no Monogatari: Story of the Cross* (1591: in Vatican Libr.).

BARR, PAT, *The Coming of the Barbarians* (London, *etc.*, Macmillan, 1967).

BERKELEY, PEPPER, Article in *The Register-Guard* (U.S.A.).

BOXER, C. R., *Jan Compagnie in Japan, 1600-1817* (The Hague, Nijhoff, 1936; rev. ed., 1950; rev. ed., Tokyo, etc., Oxford Univ. Pr., 1968), pp. 67-115 (1968 ed.).

——, *The Christian Century in Japan, 1549-1650* (Berkeley & Los Angeles, Univ. of California Pr., & London, Cambridge Univ. Pr., 1951, 1967).

——, *The Great Ship* (1959): As in V.

——, *The Dutch Seaborne Empire 1600-1800* (London, Hutchinson, 1965; Harmondsworth, Penguin, 1973).

COSTANTINI, CELSO, As in I, 1949: II, ii (pp. 233-250).

ENDO, SHUSHAKU, *Silence* (a novel) (Jap. ed., 1966; Engl. trans., Tokyo, Sophia Univ., & Tokyo & Rutland, Vt, Tuttle, 1969).

GRUNNE, FRANCOIS DE, 'Premier art chrétien japonais', in: *Art d'église* (Bruges, Abbaye de Saint-André (now Ottignies, Monastère Saint-André), III (1960, no. 2), pp. 305-313.

HILLIER, J., *Hokusai: Paintings, Drawings and Woodcuts* (Oxford, Phaidon; New York, Dutton, 1955, 1978).

HOSOMO, MASANOBU, *Nagasaki Prints and Early Copperplates* (Tokyo, *etc.*, Kodansha& Shibundo, 1978).

JANEIRA, ARMANDO MARTINS, *O Impacte Português sobre a Civilização Japanesa* (Lisboa, Publ. Dom Quixote, 1970).

JENNES, JOSEPH, *A History of the Catholic Church in Japan* (Tokyo, Oriens Inst. for Religious Research, 1973).

KAGA, ICHORO, *Christian Art of Japan during the 16th and 17th Centuries* (Kyoto, Nat. Mus. of Modern Art, 1973).

KEENE, DONALD, *The Japanese Discovery of Europe, 1720-1798* (London, Routledge & Kegan Paul, 1952; rev. & enlarged to 1830, Stanford Univ. Pr., 1969).

KIRKWOOD, K., *Renaissance in Japan: A Cultural Survey of the Seventeenth Century* (Tokyo, 1938).

LEHMANN, (E.) ARNO, As in I.

KÜCHI, MATSUDA, *The Relations between Portugal and Japan* (Lisboa, Junta de Investigações do Ultramar e Centro de Estudos Históricos Ultramarinas, 1918).

McCALL, JOHN E., 'Early Jesuit Art in the Far East', in: *Artibus Asiae* (Ascona, Sw.), x, 2, 3, 4 (1947), pp. 121-37, 216-233, 283-301.

MODI, N. A., *A Collection of Nagasaki Colour-Prints and Paintings showing the Influence of Chinese and European Art on that of Japan* (2 vols) (Kobe & London, 1939).

NISHIMURA, TEI, *Christian Art in Japan, 1549-1639: Namban Art* (Jap. text, Engl. brochure) (Tokyo, Kodansha, 1958).

OKAMOTO, YOSHITOMO, *Namban Bijutsu* (Jap.) (Tokyo, Heibonsha, 1965). Engl. trans. as: *The Namban Art of Japan* (Tokyo, Heibonsha, & New York, Weatherhill, 1972).

OTSUKI, J., *Shinsen Yogaku Nempyo* (Tokyo, 1927). Engl. trans. as: *The Infiltration of European Civilization in Japan during the 18th Century* (Leiden, 1940).

PASKE-SMITH, M. B. T., *Japanese Traditions of Christianity* (Kobe, Thompson, & London, Kegan Paul, 1930).

——, *Western Barbarians in Japan and Formosa in Tokugawa Days, 1603-1868* (Kobe, Thompson, (1930)).

RODRIGUEZ, JOÃO (ed. COOPER, MICHAEL), *This Island of Japan* (Tokyo & New York, Kodansha, 1973).

SAKAMOTO, MITSURU, & YOSHIMURA MOTOO, *Nambanbijutsu* (Jap.) (Tokyo, Shogakukan, 1974).
SANSOM, Sir G. B., *The Western World and Japan* (London, Cresset Pr., 1950, 1965).
SCHURHAMMER, G., 'Die Jesuitenmissionäre des 16. und 17. Jahrhunderts und ihre Einfluss auf die japonische Malerei', in: *Jubiläumsband 1933 der Deutschen Gesellschaft für Natur- und Völkerkunde Ostasiens*, I (Leipzig, 1934), pp. 116-126.
SHINMURA, I., *Western Influences on Japanese History and Culture in Earlier Periods (1540-1560)* (Tokyo, 1936).
STRAELEN, H. VAN, *En réfléchissant au problème de l'adaptation au Japon*: (offprint from: *Rythmes du monde* (Bruges, Abbaye de Saint-André), 1953, 2).
SULLIVAN, MICHAEL, *The Meeting of Eastern and Western Art* (London, Thames & Hudson, 1973), chaps 1, 4.
TAKENAKA, MASAO, *Seisho no Kotaba: Creation and Redemption through Japanese Art* (Jap.) (Osaka, Sogensha, 1966).
——, *Christian Art in Asia*: As in I.
TSUDA, NORITAKE, *Handbook of Japanese Art* (Tokyo, Sanseido, 1935; London, Allen & Unwin, 1937; Rutland, Vt, & Tokyo, Tuttle, 1976).
YANAGI, SOGAN, & others, *Christ through Art Works* (Jap.) (Tokyo, Kyodan Publ. Dept, 1956).

VII. THE PHILIPPINES

AHLBORN, RICHARD E., 'The Spanish Churches of Central Luzon', in: *Philippine Studies* (Manila, Ateneo), viii, 4 (Oct. 1960), pp. 802-814.
——, 'Spanish Churches of Central Luzon: The Provinces near Manila', in: *Philippine Studies* (Manila, Ateneo), xi, 2 (Apr. 1963), pp. 283-292).
CARANO, PAUL, & SANCHEZ, PEDRO C., *A Complete History of Guam* (Rutland, Vt, & Tokyo, Tuttle, 1964).
CASTAÑELA, DOMINADOR, *Art in the Philippines* (Quezon City, Univ. of the Philippines, 1964).
COSETENG, ALICIA M. L., *Spanish Churches in the Philippines* (Detroit, Cellar Book Shop, for UNESCO National Commission for the Philippines, 1972).
COSTA, H. DE LA, *The Jesuits in the Philippines, 1581-1768* (Cambridge, Mass., Harvard Univ. Pr., 1961).
DÍAZ-TRECHUELO SPINOLA, MARÍA LOURDES, *Arquitectura Española en Filipinas (1565-1800)* (Sevilla, Escuela de Estudios Hispano-Americanos, 1959).
DULDULAO, MANUEL D., *Contemporary Philippine Art* (Quezon City, Vera Reyes, 1972).
LEGARDO, Jr, BENITO, 'Colonial Churches of Ilocos', in: *Philippine Studies* (Manila, Ateneo), viii, 1 (Jan. 1960), pp. 121-158.
MARCO DORTA, ENRIQUE, *Arte en America y Filipinas* (vol. xxi in: *Ars Hispaniae*) (Madrid, Plus-Ultra, 1958, 1973), pp. 394-408, 430.
NORTON, M. M., *Guide to Manila Catholic Churches* (Manila, McCullough, 1915).
OCAMPO, GALO B., *The Religious Element in Philippine Art* (Manila, Univ. of S. Tomás, 1967).
PIÑOL, GÓMEZ, A standard work said in 1973 to be expected soon.
SMITH, WINFIELD SCOTT, *The Art of the Philippines* (Manila, 1958).
TAKENAKA, MASAO, As in I.
ZÓBEL DE AYALA, FERNANDO, *Philippine Religious Imagery* (Manila, Ateneo, 1963).

VIII. OCEANIA

ASHE, GEOFFREY, in: Ashe, Geoffrey (ed.), *The Quest for America* (London, Pall Mall Pr., 1971), pp. 277-278.
CLARKE, BASIL, F. L., As in III; chaps 8, 9.
COCHRANE, GLYNN, *Big Men and Cargo Cults* (Oxford, Clarendon Pr., 1970).
COSTANTINI, CELSO, As in I.
COUSINS, GEORGE, *The Story of the South Seas* (London, London Missionary Society, 1894), pp. 57-61.
GERMANN, GEORG, *Gothic Revival in Europe and Britain* (London, Lund Humphries, with Arch. Assoc., 1972), pp. 108-112.
HALDANE, CHARLOTTE, *Tempest over Tahiti* (London, Constable, 1963), pp. 26-27.
LAWRENCE, PETER, *Road Belong Cargo* (Manchester, Univ. Pr., 1964).
LEHMANN, (E.) ARNO, As in I.
LOVETT, R., *History of the London Missionary Society, 1795-1895* (London, Oxford Univ. Pr., 1899), i, pp. 219-231.
Missionskalender 1974 (Aachen, Missio).

NEIL, J. MEREDITH, *Paradise Improved* (Charlottesville, Univ. Pr. of Virginia, for Amer. Assoc. of Arch. Bibliographers, 1972).

Pacific Islands Monthly, May 1950, p. 85.

TAKENAKA, MASAO, As in I.

TIPPETT, A. R., *The Christian (Fiji, 1835-1867)* (Auckland, Institute Printing & Publ. Soc., n.d., after 1939).

WORSLEY, PETER, *And the Trumpet shall Sound* (London, MacGibbon & Kee, 1957; 2nd ed., Paladin, 1968).

IX. AMERICA

Abstracts of two Sessions of the Society of Architectural Historians, April 1975, in: *Journal of the Society of Architectural Historians* (Philadelphia), xxxiv, 4 (Dec. 1975), pp. 295-302.

ACUÑA, LUIS ALBERTO, *Diccionario Biográfico de Artistas que trabajaron en el Nuevo Reino de Granada* (Bogotá, Instituto Colombiano de Cultura Hispánica, 1964).

——, *Les Artes en Colombia: 3: La Escultura* (vol. xx of *Historia Extensa de Colombia*) (Bogotá, Lerner, 1967).

AHLBORN, RICHARD E., *Saints of San Xavier* (Tuscon, Arizona, Southwestern Mission Research Center, 1974).

ALTAMIRA, LUIS ROBERTO, *Córdoba, sus Pintores y sus Pinturas* (2 vols) (Córdoba, Arg., Imp. Univ., 1954).

ANDERS, FERDINAND; MAZA, DE LA, FRANCISCO; CASTELLÓ YTURBIDE & TERESA MARTÍNEZ DEL RÍO DE REDO, Marita; *Tesores de México: Arte Plumario y de Mosaico* (Span., Engl., Germ.) (México, D.F., *Artes de México*, No. 137, 1970).

ANDRADE, R. F. M. DE, 'Contribuição para o Estudo da Obra do Aleijadhinho', in: *Revista de Serviço do Patrimônio Histórico e Artístico* (Rio de Janeiro), 2 (1938), pp. 255-259.

ÁNGULO IÑIGUEZ, DIEGO, 'El Gótico y el Renacimiento en las Antillas', in: *Anuario de Estudios Americanos* (Sevilla, Escuela de Estudios Hispano-Americanos), iv (1947).

——, *Historia del Arte Hispanoamericano*, I (Barcelona, Salvat, 1945, 1955).

ÁNGULO IÑIGUEZ, DIEGO; DORTA, E. MARCO, & BUSCHIAZZO, MARÍO J., *Historia del Arte Hispanoamericano* (7 vols) (Barcelona, Salvat, 1945/56).

Anon., Ac. Nac. de Bellas Artes: *El Templo de San Ignacio* (Buenos Aires, Peuser, 1947).

——, *Antiguas Iglesias y Capillas de Chile: Ancient Churches and Chapels of Chile* (Calendar: Span. & Engl.) (Ed. Lord Cochrane, 1975).

——, *Antonio Francisco Lisboa, O Aleijadinho* (Rio de Janeiro, Min. de Educ. e Saudo, 1953).

——, *Aspectos de Arquitectura Barroco Luso-Brasileiro* (Cat. of an Exhib.) (Lisboa, Fund. Gulbenkian, 1968).

——, *Arte Colonial en Santo Domingo Siglos XVI-XVIII: Exposición* (Rep. Dom., Univ. of Santo Domingo, n.d.).

——, *Arte Religiosa Popular do Novo México* (Exhib. Cat.) (Lisboa, Museu Nac. de Arte Antiga, 1957).

——, *Barroco Brasileiro* (Exhib. Cat.) (Lisboa, Fund. Gulbenkian, 1973).

——, *Cuzco: Reconstruction of the Town and Restoration of its Monuments* (Paris, UNESCO, 1956).

——, *Exposición de Arte ... 300 Años de Arte en Cuba* (La Habana, Univ., n.d.).

——, *Handlist of the Collection of The Spanish Colonial Arts Society, Inc.* (? Santa Fe, N.M., ? 1953).

——, *Kamaq* (Span. & Engl.) (? Cuzco, Artesianas del Perú, ? 1972).

——, *La Arquitectura Mestiza en las Riberas del Titikaca* (Buenos Aires, Ac. Nac. de Bellas Artes, 1952).

——, *Les Iglesias de Potosí* (Buenos Aires, Ac. Nac. de Bellas Artes, 1945).

——, *Platería Mexicana* (Span. & Engl.) (México, D.F., Museo Nat. de Artes e Industrias Populares, 1952).

——, *Pintura Brasileira*, I (Rio de Janeiro, Inst. Bras. de Educ., Ciência e Cultura, Comissão Nacional de UNESCO, 1952).

——, *Rutas Históricas de la Arquitectura Virreinal Altoperuana* (Buenos Aires, Ac. Nac. de Bellas Artes, 1958).

——, *South American Country Art* (Cat. of Exhib. at Tooth & Portal Galleries, London, 1970/1).

——, *Three Centuries of Mexican Colonial Architecture* (Span. & Engl.) (New York & London, Appleton-Century, for Dept of Educ., Rep. Mex., 1933).

——, *Tres Siglos de Pintura Venezolana* (Caracas, Museo de Bellas Artes, 1943).

ARANGO, JORGE, & MARTINEZ, CARLOS, *Arquitectura en Colombia, Arquitectura Colonial 1538-1810* (Bogotá, Proa, 1951).

Artes de México (México, D.F., monthly, 1954 on). Esp. xxi. 182/3, *La Catedral de México*.

BACHMANN, KURT, and others, *Popular Paintings from Haiti* (Exhib. Cat.) (London, Arts Council, 1968).

BAER, KURT & RUDINGER, HUGO, *Architecture of the California Missions* (Berkeley & Los Angeles, Univ. of California Pr., 1958).

——, 'California Indian Art', in: *The Americas*, xvi. 1 (July 1959), pp. 23-44.

BAIRD, J. A., Jr, *The Churches of Mexico, 1530-1810* (Berkeley & Los Angeles, Univ. of California Pr., 1962).

BARDI, PIETRO MARIA, *New Brazilian Art* (New York, etc., Praeger Publ., 1970).

BARTLETT, LANIER, *Carved Ornamentation of the California Mission Period* (Los Angeles, S. California Index of Amer. Design, Works Progress Admin., 1940).

——, *Mission Motifs: A Collection of Decorative Details from Old Missions of California* (same publ.).

BAZIN, GERMAIN, *L'architecture religieuse baroque au Brésil* (São Paulo, Museu de Arte, & Paris, Plon, 1956 (vol. i), 1958 (vol. ii)).

——, *L'Aleijadinho et la sculpture baroque au Brésil* (Paris, Le Temps, 1963).

——, *Baroque and Rococo* (London, Thames & Hudson, 1964, 1974). Earlier Fr. ed.

BENEVIDES, ALFREDO, *La Arquitectura en el Virreinato del Perú y en la Capitanía General de Chile* (Santiago, Enillos, 1941).

BLASCO, ROBERTO (ed.), *Arte de Venezuela* (Caracas, Univ. Central de Ven., 1959).

Boletín del Centro de Investigaciones Históricas y Estéticas (Caracas, Fac. de Arqu. y Urbanismo, Univ. Central de Venezuela): Nos 1-23, Jan. 1964 - Jan. 1978.

BOTTINEAU, YVES, *Living Architecture: Iberian-American Baroque* (London Macdonald, 1971; Engl. trans. of Fr. ed., Fribourg, Office du Livre, 1970).

BOULTON, ALFREDO, *Historia de la Pintura en Venezuela: I: Época Colonial* (Caracas, Arte, 1964, 1968, 1971).

——, *Historia Abreviada de la Pintura en Venezuela: I: Época Colonial* (Caracas, Monte Avila, 1971).

BOYD, E., *The Literature of Santos* (Dallas, Southern Methodist Univ. Pr., 1950); reprinting an article in *Southwest Review*, 1950.

——, *Popular Arts of Spanish New Mexico* (Santa Fe, Mus. of New Mexico Pr., 1974).

——, *Saints and Saint-makers of New Mexico*.

——, *The New Mexico Santero*.

BRENNER, ANITA, *Idols behind Altars* (New York, 1929).

BRUGHETTI, ROMUALDO, *Introdución al Estudio de la Escuela Pictórica Argentina* (Buenos Aires, Dirección General de Relaciones Culturales, 1964).

——, *Historia del Arte en Argentina* (México, D.F., Pormaca, 1965).

BUNTING, BAINBRIDGE, *Taos Adobes: Spanish Colonial and Territorial Architecture of the Taos Valley* (Santa Fe, Univ. of New Mexico Pr., 1964).

——, *Of Earth and Timbers Made: New Mexico Architecture* (Albuquerque, Univ. of New Mexico Pr., 1974).

——, *Early Architecture in New Mexico* (Albuquerque, Univ. of New Mexico Pr., 1977).

BURLAND, COTTIE A., 'The Church in South America', in: Frere-Cook, Gervis (ed.): As in I: chap. 11 (pp. 221-236).

BURY, JOHN B., 'The Aleijadinho', in: *The Cornhill Magazine* (London, Murray), 979 (Summer 1949), pp. 69-80.

——, 'The Twelve Prophets at Congonhas do Campo', in: *The Month* (London, Longmans Green) ii, 3 (Sept. 1949), pp. 152-171.

——, 'The "Borrominesque" Churches of Colonial Brazil'; reprint from: *Art Bulletin* (College Art Assoc. for America), xxxvii, 1 (March 1955), pp. 28-53.

BUSCHIAZZO, MARÍO J., *La Arquitectura Colonial en Hispano-America* (Buenos Aires, Soc. Cent. de Arquitectos, 1940).

——, *La Catedral de Buenos Aires* (Buenos Aires, La Mundial, 1943).

——, *Estudios de Arquitectura Colonial Hispano-Americana* (Buenos Aires, Kraft, 1944).

——, 'Exotic Influences in American Colonial Art', in: *Journal of the Society of Architectural Historians* (Philadelphia), v (1946/7), pp. 21-23.

——, *Historia de la Arquitectura en Iberoamerica* (Buenos Aires, Emmecé, 1963).

CALI, FRANÇOIS, *L'art des Conquistadors* (Paris, D. Arthaud, 1960). Engl. trans., as: *The Art of the Conquistadors* (London, Thames & Hudson, 1961).

CAMACHO, C. A., 'El Templo de la Compañia de Bogotá', in: *Boletín*, as above, 6 (Sept. 1966), pp. 86-104.

CAMACHO, LUIS ALBERTO, *Les Artes en Colombia: 4: La Arquitectura Colonial* (vol. xx of *Historia Extensa de Colombia*) (Bogotá, Lerner, 1967).

CAMERON, PHILIP, *The Lost Paradise* (London, Sidgwick, 1975).

CAMERON, RODERICK, *Viceroyalties of the West: The Spanish Empire in Latin America* (London, Weidenfeld & Nicolson, 1968).

CAMPEN, RICHARD N., *Architecture of the Western Reserve: 1800-1900* (Cleveland & London, Case Western Reserve Univ. Pr., 1971).

CARRILLO Y GARIEL, ABELARDO, *Técnica de la Pintura de Nueva España* (México, D.F., Imp. Univ., 1946).

——, *Imaginería Popular Novoespañola* (México, D.F., Ed. Mexicanas, 1950).

CASTEDO, LEOPOLDO, *A History of Latin American Art and Architecture* (London, Pall Mall Pr., 1969); in Span. as: *Historia del Arte y de la Arquitectura Latinoamericana* (Barcelona, Poimare, 1970).

CERNY, CHARLENE, *Navajo Pictorial Weaving* (Santa Fe, Museum of International Folk Art, 1975).

CHARLOT, JEAN, *Mexican Art and the Academy of San Carlos: 1785-1915* (Austin, Univ. of Texas Pr., 1962).

CHASE, GILBERT, *Contemporary Art in Latin America* (New York, Free Pr., & London, Collier-Macmillan, 1970).

CINADER, BERNHARD, *Contemporary Native Art of Canada: The Woodland Indians* (Cat. of an Exhib. at Lahr and London, 1976).

CORRUJO FRANCO, JOSÉ, *Guadalajara Colonial* (México, D.F., Consejo de Colaboración Municipal de Guadalajara, 1970).

COSTA, LUCIO, *Arquitectura Brasileira* (Rio de Janeiro, Min. de Educ. e Sauda, 1952).

COSTANTINI, CELSO, 1949: As in I.

DAMAZ, PAUL F., *Art in Latin American Architecture* (New York, Reinhold, 1963).

DEWDNEY, SELWYN, *The Sacred Scrolls of the Southern Ojibway* (Toronto & Buffalo, Univ. of Toronto Pr., for the Glenbow-Alberta Inst., Calgary, 1975).

DORNER, GERD, *Mexican Folk-Art* (Munich & Vienna, Andermann, 1962).

EDMONSON, MUNRO S.; CORREA, GUSTAVO; THOMPSON, DONALD E.; MADSEN, WILLIAM, *Nativism and Syncretism* (New Orleans, Middle American Research Institute, Tulane Univ., 1960).

ELDER, PAUL, *The Old Spanish Missions of California* (San Francisco, Elder, 1913).

El Palacio (Santa Fe, Univ. of New Mexico, 1918 on).

ESPINOSA, JOSÉ E., *Saints in the Valleys*.

FERNÁNDEZ, JUSTINO, *Arte Mexicana de sus Orígines a nuestras Días* (México, D.F., Porrúa, 2nd ed., 1961). Engl. trans. as: *A Guide to Mexican Art* (Chicago & London, Univ. of Chicago Pr., 1969), pp. 53-120 (of Engl. ed.).

——, *Mexican Art* (Feltham, Hamlyn, 1965, rev. ed. 1967, 1970).

FIRPI, JOSÉ, *El Arte de la Imaginería Popular en Puerto Rico: The Art of Folk Imagery in Puerto Rico* (Span. & Engl.) (San Juan, P.R., Ed. Tau, or Author at 52 King's Court, Santurce, P.R., 00911, 1973).

FLORES GUERRERO, R., *Las Capillas Posas de México* (México, D.F., Ed. Mexicanas, 1951).

FONSECA BRANCANTE, ELDINO DA, *O Brasil e a Louça de Índia* (São Paulo, Kosmos, 1950).

FREUDENFELD, R. A., *Mestre Antonio Francisco, O Aleijadinho* (São Paulo, Ed. Inteligencia, ? 1940).

FURLONG, GUILLERMO, *Arquitectos Argentinos durante la Dominación Hispánica* (Buenos Aires, Huarpes, 1946).

——, *Artesanos Argentinos durante la Dominación Hispánica* (Buenos Aires, Huarpes, 1946).

GARCÍA GRANADOS, R., 'Reminiscencias Idolátricas en Monumentos Coloniales', in: *Anales del Instituto de Investigaciones Estéticas*, iii (1940), pp. 54-56.

GASPARINI, GRAZIANO, *Templos Coloniales de Venezuela* (Caracas, Ed. 'A', 1959).

——, 'Analisis Crítico de la Historiografía Arquitectónica del Barroco en América', in: *Boletín*, as above, 7 (Apr. 1967), pp. 9-29.

——, 'Observaciones en Willka Waman', in: *Boletín*, as above, 18 (Apr., 1974), pp. 93-116.

GIRALDO JARAMILLO, GABRIEL, *La Pintura en Colombia* (México, D.F., Fondo de Cultura Económica, 1948).

GISBERT, TERESA, 'Creación de Estructuras Arquitectónicas y Urbanas en la Sociedad Virreinal', in: *Boletín*, as above, 22 (Jan. 1977), pp. 125-176.

GOODMAN, EDWARD J., *The Explorers of South America* (New York, Macmillan, & London, Collier-Macmillan, 1972).

GUIDO, ANGEL, *Estimativa Moderna de la Pintura Colonial* (Rosario, Arg., Ac. Nac. de la Historia, 1942).

HARTEZ, JÜRGEN, & SCHMIDT, KATHARINA, *Barocke Malerei aus den Anden* (Cat. of an Exhib.) (Düsseldorf, Stadtischen Kunsthalle, 1976).

HARVEY, JOHN, *The Gothic World* (London, etc., Batsford, 1950).

HAYES, ALDEN C., *The Four Churches of Pecos* (Albuquerque, Univ. of New Mexico Pr., 1974).

HEIKAMP, DETLEF, and ANDERS, FERDINAND, *Mexico and the Medici* (Engl. & Ital.) (Florence, Edam, 1972).

HERNANDEZ DE ALBA, GUILLERMO, *Arte Hispánico en Colombia* (Bogotá, Dirección de Información y Propaganda del Estado, 1955).

——, *Les Artes en Colombia: I: La Pintura en el Nuevo Reino de Granada* (vol. xx of *Historia Extensa de Colombia*) (Bogotá, Lerner, 1967).

HERNÁNDEZ PERERA, JESÚS, *Sobre los Arquitectos de la Catedral de Las Palmas, 1500-1570* (Las Palmas, El Museo Canario, 1960) (*sep. de El Museo Canario*, 73/74 (1960)).

HEWETT, EDGAR L., & FISHER, REGINALD D., *Mission Monuments of New Mexico* (Albuquerque, Univ. of New Mexico Pr., 1942).

Hojas de Cultura Popular Colombiana (Bogotá, Presidencia de la República, 1951 on).

HOLWAY, MARY GORDON, *Art of the Old World in New Spain and the Mission Days of Alta California* (San Francisco, A. M. Robertson, 1922).

JAMES, GEORGE WHARTON, *In and Out of the Old Missions of California* (Boston, Little, Brown, 1905).

JORGE, FERNANDO, *Notas sôbre O Aleijadinho* (São Paulo, Sociedade Impressora Brasileira, 1951).

KELEMEN, PÁL, *Baroque and Rococo in Latin America* (New York, Macmillan, 1951; rev. ed. (2 vols), New York, Dover Publ., 1967).

——, *Art of the Americas, Ancient and Hispanic* (New York, Thomas Y. Crowell Co., 1969).

KILHAM, WALTER H., *Mexican Architecture of the Vice-Regal Period* (New York & London, Longmans, 1927).

KING, PATRICK, *Pueblo Indian Religious Architecture* (Salt Lake City, Univ. of Utah, 1977).

KINGMAN, EDUARDO, *Guia del Museo de Arte Colonial* (Quito, Casa de la Cultura Ecuatoriana, 1951).

KRULL, GERMAINE, *Ouro Préto* (Lisboa, Ed. Atlântico, 1943).

KUBLER, GEORGE, *The Religious Architecture of New Mexico* (Colorado Springs, Taylor Mus., 1940; 4th ed., Albuquerque, Univ. of New Mexico Pr., 1972).

——, *Mexican Architecture of the Sixteenth Century* (New Haven, Yale Univ. Pr., 1941).

KUBLER, GEORGE, & SORÍA, MARTIN, *Art and Architecture in Spain and Portugal and their American Dominions* (Baltimore, 1958; Harmondsworth, Penguin, 1959).

LA FARGE, OLIVER, *Santa Eulalia: The Religion of a Cuchumatau Indian Town* (Chicago, 1947).

LAROCHE, W. E., *Los Precursores y otras Fuentes Documentales para nuestra Iconografia Pictórica* (Montevideo, Museo y Archivo Ernesto Larroche, 1961).

——, *La Pintura de El Uraguay* (Montevideo, Museo y Archivo Ernesto Larroche, 1963).

LIBRARY OF CONGRESS, Historical American Buildings Survey: Plans of 16 California Missions.

LIPMAN, JEAN, & WINCHESTER, ALICE, *The Flowering of American Folk Art: 1776-1876*: Catalogue of an Exhibition (New York, Viking Pr., with Whitney Mus. of Amer. Art, & Canada, Macmillan Co. of Canada, & London, Thames & Hudson, 1974).

LOPES, FRANCISCO ANTONIO, *História da Construçao da Igreja do Carmo do Ouro Préto* (Rio de Janeiro, Min. de Educ. e Saude, 1942).

LOZOYA, MARQUÉS DE, *Historia del Arte Hispánico*, IV, chaps viii-x (Barcelona, Salvat, 1945).

LUJÁN MUÑOZ, JORGE, Review of Markman 1966, in: *Journal of the Society of Architectural Historians* (Philadelphia), xxvii, 1 (March 1968), pp. 88-92.

LUZBETAK, LOUIS J., As in I.

MACHADO DE CARVALHO, P. A., *Antiguidades Brasileiras* (Rio de Janeiro, Alvaro, 1965).

MANN, HANS & GRACIELA, *The Twelve Prophets of Aleijadinho* (photos) (Austin & London, Univ. of Texas Pr., 1967).

MARCO DORTA, ENRIQUE, *Fuentes para la Historia del Arte Hispanoamericano* (2 vols) (Sevilla, Inst. Diego Velázquez, 1960).

——, *Arte en America y Filipinas*: As in VII.

MARIANNO FILHO, JOSÉ, *Influencias Muçulmanas na Architectura Tradicional Brasileira* (Rio de Janeiro, Noite, 1943).

——, *Aspectos de Arquitectura Barroco Luso-Brasileira*.

——, *A. F. Lisbôa* (Rio de Janeiro, Serviço do Patrimônio Histórico, 1945; São Paulo, Melhoramentos, 1961).

MARIÁTEGUI OLIVA, RICARDO, *Escultura Colonial de Trujillo* (Lima, Alma Mater, 1946).

MARKMAN, SIDNEY D., *O Aleijadinho* (São Paulo, Melhoramentos, 3rd ed. 1961).

——, *Colonial Architecture of Antigua Guatemala* (Philadelphia, Amer. Phil Soc., 1966).

——, 'Pre-Columbian Survivals in Colonial Hispano-American Art and Architecture', in: *Boletín*, as above, 19 (Dec. 1974), pp. 43-56.

MAZA, FRANCISCO DE LA, *Los Retablos Dorados de Nueva España* (México D.F., Ed. Mexicanas, No. 9, 1950).

——, *La Ciudad de Cholula e sus Iglesias* (Mexico D.F., Univ., Inst. de Investigaciones Estéticas, 1959).

——, *La Mitología Clasica en el Arte Colonial de México* (México D.F., Univ., Inst. de Invest. Est., 1968).

——, *El Arte Colonial en San Luis Potasí* (México D.F., Univ., Inst. de Invest. Est., 1969).

MAZA, FRANCISCO DE LA; PARDINAS, FELIPE; ENCIMA, JUAN DE LA; ORTEZ MUCEDO, LUIS; & MOYSSEI, XAVIER, *Cuarenta Siglos do Plástica Mexicana* (México D.F., Hermes, 1970).

McANDREW, JOHN, *The Open-Air Churches of Sixteenth-Century Mexico* (Cambridge, Mass., Harvard Univ. Pr., 1965).

McCALL, JOHN E., As in V: x, 4 (1947), p. 299.

MEIRELES, CECILIA, *Artes Populares* (Rio de Janeiro, Ed. de Ouro, 1968).

MESA, JOSÉ DE, & GISBERT, TERESA, *Holguin y la Pintura Altoperuana del Virreinato* (La Paz, Bibl. Paceña, 1956).

——, *Iglesias con Atrio y Posas en Bolivia* (La Paz, Ac. Nac. de Ciencias de Bol., 1961).

——, *Contribuciones al Estudio de la Arquitectura Andina* (La Paz, Ac. Nac. de Ciencias de Bolivia, 1966).

——, *El Arte en Perú y Bolivia* (1800-1840) (La Paz, Univ., Fac. de Fil. y Letras, 1966).

Monumentos Históricos y Arqueológicos de América (México D.F., Inst. Panamericano de Geografía y Historia, Comisión de Historia, 1950 on).

MORISON, SAMUEL ELIOT, *The European Discovery of America* (New York & London, Oxford Univ. Pr., 1971).

NAVARRO, JOSÉ GABRIEL, *La Escultura en el Ecuador* (*Siglos XVI al XVIII*) (Madrid, Real Ac. de Bellas Artes de San Fernando, 1929).

——, *La Iglesia de la Compañia en Quito* (Madrid, Antonio Marzo, 1930).

——, *Artes Plásticas Ecuatorianas* (México D.F., Fondo de Cultura Económica, 1945).

——, *El Arte en la Provincia del Quito* (México D.F., Inst. Panamericano de Geografía e Historia, 1960).

NEGRO, CARLOS DEL, *Contribução ao Estudo da Pintura Mineira* (Rio de Janeiro, Diretoria de Patrimônio Histórico e Artistico Nacional, 1958).

NEUERBURG, NORMAN, 'Painting in the California Missions', in: *American Art Review*, 4. 1 (July 1977), pp. 72-88.

NEUMAYER, ALFRED, 'The Indian Contribution to Architectural Decoration in Spanish Colonial America', in: *Art Bulletin*, xxx (1948), pp. 104-121.

NEWCOMB, REXFORD, *The Franciscan Mission Architecture of Alta California* (New York, Architectural Book Publ. Co., 1916; rev. ed., New York, Dover Publ., 1973).

——, *The Old Mission Churches and Historic Houses of California: Their History, Architecture, Art and Lore* (Philadelphia, Lipincott, 1925).

——, *Spanish-Colonial Architecture in the United States* (New York, J. J. Augustin, 1937).

NOEL, MARTÍN S., *Contribución a la Historia de la Arquitectura Hispano-Americano* (Buenos Aires, Peuser, 1921).

——, *Teoría Histórica de la Arquitectura Virreinal* (Buenos Aires, Peuser, 1932).

——, *Estudios y Documentos para la Historia del Arte Colonial, I, Arquitectura Virreinal* (Buenos Aires, Inst. de Investigaciones Históricas, 1934).

——, *El Arte en la America Española* (Buenos Aires, Peuser, 1942).

NOEL, MARTÍN S., & others, *La Villa Imperial de Potosí* (Buenos Aires, Nac. Acad. de Bellas Artes, 1943).

OAKES, MAUD, *The Two Crosses of Todos Santos: Survivals of Mayan Religious Ritual* (New York, Pantheon Books, for Bollingen Found., 1951, 1969).

OBER, FREDERICK, *Travels in Mexico and Life among the Indians* (Boston, Mass., Estes & Lauriat, 1884; London & Cambridge, Mass., Warner, 1890).

OLVERA, JORGE, *Artes de México*, vol. v, año vii, no. 32, *La Catedral Metropolitana*.

OSBORNE, LILLY DE JONGHE, *Indian Crafts of Guatemala and El Salvador* (Norman, Univ. of Oklahoma Pr., 1965).

PALM, ERWIN WALTER, 'Las Capillas Abiertas Americanas y sus Antecedentes en el Occidente Cristiano', in: *Anales de Arte Americano y Investigaciones Estéticas* (Buenos Aires), 6 (1953), pp. 47-64.

——, *Los Monumentos Arquitectónicos de la Española* (2 vols) (Trujillo, Univ. of Santo Domingo, 1955).

——, 'El Arte del Nuevo Mundo despues de la Conquista Española', in: *Boletín*, as above, 4 (Jan. 1966), pp. 37-50.

PEREIRA SALAS, EUGENIO, *Historia del Arte en el Reino de Chile* (Santiago, Univ. de Chile, 1965).
PEREZNIETO CASTRO, FERNANDO, *Conventos del Siglo XVI* (Span. & Engl.) (México D.F., Mortiz, 1976).
PETTERSON, RICHARD, *Folk Art of Peru* (Claremont, Cal., Author, 1968).
PICOŃ-SALAS, MARIANO, *De la Conquista a la Independencia* (México D.F., Fondo de Cultura Económica, 1944; 3rd ed., 1958). Engl. trans. as: *A Cultural History of Spanish America* (Berkeley & Los Angeles, Univ. of California Pr., 1962).
——, *La Pintura en Venuzuela* (Caracas, Secretaría General de la Décima Conferencia Interamericana, 1954).
PINHEIRO, SILVANISIO, *Azulejos do Convento de S. Francisco in Bahia* (Salvador-Bahia, Livria Turistá, 1951).
PINZANO RESTREPO, ROBERTO, *Gregório Vazquez de Arce y Cebala* (Paris, Camilo Block, 1946).
PIO, FERNANDO, *Roteiro de Arte Sacra* (Cat. of an Exhib. at Recife, 1960) (Min. de Educ. e Cult.).
PLÁ, JOSEPHINA, *El Templo de Yaguarón* (Asunción, Ed. do Centenario, 1970).
PLATTNER, F. A., *Deutsche Meister des Barock in Südamerika* (Basel, Herder, 1960).
POHL, FREDERICK J., *The Viking Settlements of North America* (New York, Potter, 1972).
PRAT-PUIG, F., *Pre-Barroco en Cuba: Una Escuela Criolla de Arquitectura Morisca* (Havana, 1947).
QUIRARTE, JACINTO, *Mexican American Artists* (Austin & London, Univ. of Texas Pr., 1973), pp. 16-30.
REIS, JOSÉ MARIA DOS, *História da Pintura no Brasil* (São Paulo, 1944).
RODMAN, SELDEN, *Renaissance in Haiti* (New York, Pellegrini & Cudahy, 1948).
——, *Haiti: The Black Republic* (New York, later Old Greenwich, Conn., 1954, 1955, rev. ed. 1961, rev. ed. 1973), pp. 61-105 of 1973 ed.
RODRIGUEZ, ANTONIO, *Der Mensch in Flammen: Wändermalerei in Mexiko* (Dresden, Verlag der Kunst, 1967). Engl. trans. as: *A History of Mexican Mural Painting* (London, Thames & Hudson, 1969), pp. 92-145 of Engl. ed.
ROJAS, PEDRO, *Tonantzintla* (México D.F., Univ. Pr., 1956).
——, *Historia General del Arte Mexicano: II: Época Colonial* (México D.F. & Buenos Aires, Hermes, 1963).
——, *The Art and Architecture of Mexico* (Feltham, Hamlyn, 1968).
ROMERA, ANTONIO R., *Historia de la Pintura Chilena* (Santiago de Chile, Ed. del Pacifico, 1951).
ROMERO DE TERRORES, MANUEL, *El Arte en México durante el Virreinato: Resumen Histórico* (México D.F., Porrúa, 1951).
ROOSEVELT, ANDRÉ, *Quito Churches: 48 Original Photographs* (Quito, Gutemberg, 1939).
ROUSELL, AAGE, 'Farms and Churches in the Mediaeval Norse Settlements in Greenland', in: *Meddeleser om Grønland* (København), 89, 1 (1941).
ROYS, RALPH L., *The Book of Chilam Balam of Chumayel* (Washington D.C., Carnegie Inst., 1933; Norman, Univ. of Oklahoma Pr., 1969).
RUBENS, CARLOS, *The History of Painting in Brazil* (Rio de Janeiro, Min. for Foreign Affairs, 1943).
RUBIN DE LA BORBOLLA, DANIEL F., *Las Artes Populares Indígenas de América: Supervivencia y Fomento* (Recife, Sudene-Divisão de Documentação, 1963).
RUBIO, ANGEL, *La Ciudad de Panamá* (Panamá, Banco de Urbanicación y Rehabilitación, 1950).
SANFORD, TRENT ELWOOD, *The Story of Architecture in Mexico* (New York, Norton, 1947).
SANTOS, *O Barroco e o Jesuitico do Brasil* (Rio de Janeiro, 1951).
SANTOS, FRANCISCO, Marquês de, *Louça e Porcelana* (Rio de Janeiro, Ed. de Ouro, 1968).
SANTOS, REINALDO DOS, *Antecedentes Portuguéses e Exóticos* (Rio de Janeiro, Ed. de Ouro, 1968).
SANTOS SIMÕES, J. M. DOS, *Azulejaria Portuguesa no Brasil (1500-1822)* (Lisboa, Fund. Gulbenkian, 1965).
SCHURZ, WILLIAM LYTLE, *The Manila Galleon* (New York, Dutton, 1939, 1959).
SEBASTIÁN, SANTIAGO, 'La Decoración llamada Platersca en el Mundo Hispánico', in: *Boletín*, as above, 6 (Sept. 1966), pp. 42-85.
SINNOTT, EDMUND W., *Meeting House and Church in Early New England* (New York, etc., McGraw-Hill, 1963).
SITWELL, SACHEVERELL, *Southern Baroque Revisited* (London, Weidenfeld & Nicolson, 1967), pp. 201-202.
SMITH, FRANCIS RAND, *The Architectural History of Mission San Carlos Borromeo, California* (Berkeley, Calif. Hist. Survey Commission, 1921).
——, *The Mission of San Antonio de Padua (California)* (Stanford Univ., Univ. Pr., 1932).
——, 'The Mission of Nuestra Señora de la Soledad', in: *California Hist. Soc. Qu.*, 23 (1944), pp. 1-18.
SMITH, ROBERT C., *As Artes no Bahia* (Salvador, 1944).

——, *The Colonial Art of Latin America: A Collection of Slides and Photographs* (Washington, U.S. Govt Office, 1945).

——, *Arquitectura Colonial Bahiana* (Bahia, Museu do Estado, 1951).

——, 'Nossa Senhora da Conceição da Praia and the Joanine Style in Brazil', in: *Journal of the Society of Architectural Historians* (Philadelphia), xv, 3 (Oct. 1956), pp. 16-23.

SMITH, ROBERT C., & WILDER, ELIZABETH, *A Guide to the Art of Latin America* (Washington, Libr. of Congress, 1948).

TONEYAMA, KOJIN & ESPESEL CARLOS, *The Popular Arts of Mexico* (New York, Weatherhill, & London, Phaidon, 1974).

TOUSSAINT, MANUEL, *Tasco* (Mexico D.F., Ed. Cultural, 1931).

——, *Patzcuaro* (México D.F., Inst. de Invest. Estéticas, 1942).

——, *Arte Mudéjar en América* (México D.F., Porrúa, 1946).

——, *Arte Colonial en México* (México D.F., Imp. Univ., 1948, 1962, 1974). Engl. trans. as: *Colonial Art in Mexico* (Austin & London, Univ. of Texas Pr., 1967).

——, *La Catedral de México y el Sagrario Metropolitano: Su Historia, su Tesoro, su Arte* (México D.F., Comisión Diocesana de Orden y Decoro, 1948; 2nd ed., Porrúa, 1973).

——, *Pintura Colonial en México* (México D.F., Imp. Univ., Inst. de Invest. Est., 1965).

TOUSSAINT, MANUEL, & others, *Iglesias de México* (6 vols) (México D.F., Sec. de Hacienda, 1924/5).

TRINIDADE, CÔNEGO RAIMUNDO, *São Francisco de Assis de Ouro Prêto* (Rio de Janeiro, Min. da Educ. e Saude, 1951).

VALLADERES, JOSÉ GISELLE, *Ourvesaria* (Rio de Janeiro, Ed. de Ouro, 1958).

VARGAS, JOSÉ MARIA, *El Arte Quiteno en los Siglos XVI, XVII y XVIII* (Quito, Romero, 1949).

——, *Arte Religioso Ecuatoriano* (Quito, Casa de la Cultura Ecuatoriana, 1955).

——, *Los Maestros del Arte Ecuatoriano* (Quito, Imprenta Municipal, 1960).

——, *El Arte Ecuatoriano* (Pueblo, México, Ed. J. M. Cajica Jr, 1959).

VARGAS LUGO, ELISA, *La Iglesia de Santa Prisca de Taxco* (México D.F., Univ., Inst. de Invest. Est., 1974).

Various, *Album de las Pinturas del Convento de San Francisco de Santiago* (Zürich, Moulinette, 1971).

——, 'Art of the Americas', in: *Art News Annual* (New York, Art Review Annual), xiii (1948).

——, *Journal of the Society of Architectural Historians* (Philadelphia), v (1946/7).

——, *Latin American Art and the Baroque Period in Europe* (Acts of 20th Internat. Congr. of Hist. of Art, 1961, III) (Princeton, Univ. Pr., 1963).

——, *The Art of Chile* (*The Studio* (London), May 1956).

VASCONCELLOS, SYLVIO DE, 'Introducción al Estudio del Barroco de la Región Aurifera Brasileña', in: *Boletín*, as above, 5 (May 1966), pp. 9-50.

VELARDE, HECTOR, *Arquitectura Peruana* (México D.F., Fundo de Cultura Económica, 1946).

VIDLER, VIRGINIA, *American Indian Antiques: Arts and Artefacts of the Northeast* (S. Brunswick & New York, A. S. Barnes & Co.; London, Thomas Yoseloff; 1976).

VIGIL, CARLOS, *Los Monumentos y Lugares Históricos de la Argentina* (Buenos Aires, Atlantida, 1948).

WACHTEL, NATHAN, *La vision des vaincus: Les Indiens du Pérou devant la conquête espagnol 1530-1570* (Paris, Gallimard, 1971). Engl. trans. as: *The Vision of the Vanquished* (Hassocks, Harvester Pr., 1975).

WALLACE, BIRGITTA L., 'Some Points of Controversy', in: Ashe, Geoffrey (ed.), as in VIII 1, chap. 5 (pp. 155-174).

WAX, MARVIN, *Mystique of the Missions* (Palo Alto, Cal., American West Publ. Co., 1974).

WEBB, EDITH BUCKLAND, *Indian Life at the Old Missions* (Los Angeles, Warren F. Lewis, 1952).

WETHEY, HAROLD, *Colonial Architecture and Sculpture in Peru* (Cambridge, Mass., Harvard Univ. Pr., 1949).

WILDER, MITCHELL A., and BREITENBACH, EDGAR, *Santos: The Religious Folk Art of New Mexico.*

WOLFE, MICHAEL, 'Norse Archaeology in Greenland since World War II', in: *American-Scandinavian Review*, xliv, 4 (1961/2), pp. 380-390.

WRIGHT, LOUIS B.; TATUM, GEORGE B.; MC COUBREY, JOHN W.; & SMITH, ROBERT C.; *The Arts in America: Colonial Period* (New York, Charles Scribner's Sons, 1966).

ZALVÍDAR, SERGIO G., *Arquitectura Barroco Popular, I* (México D.F., Jalisco en el Arte, 1966).

ZAPATERO, JUAN MANUEL, 'Puerto Cabello, Plaza Fuerte del Sistema Abaluartado en América', in: *Boletín* (as above), 20 (June 1975), pp. 109-141.

ZAWISZA, LESZEK M., 'Tradición Monástica Europea en los Conventos Mexicanos del Siglo XVI', in: *Boletín*, as above, 11 (May 1969), pp. 90-122.

INTRODUCTION

I. *General*

The year A.D. 1500 is not an arbitrary date in the history of Christian art. It is, roughly, the date at which Europe at last became solidly Christian; at which the rest of the world, temporally, was entirely non-Christian; at which Europe suddenly exploded outward into the rest of the world; and thereby it is also the date at which the rest of the world began (or in some cases began again) to share in Christianity and in Christian art.

Europe and Christendom had not been co-terminate till just before 1500. In its very earliest days, Christianity had been a Palestinian sect; quickly it became, and remained for some centuries, the religion of the Mediterranean basin. Then it lost the Levant and the North African littoral to Islām; however, it was meanwhile pushing northwards through Britain, North Germany, Scandinavia and Russia; and thus by late mediaeval times it was all Christian, except for the continual presence of a small Jewish *diaspora* and an atavistic witchcraft-cult, and for considerable Islāmic holdings in the Balkans and Southern Spain. With the conquest in 1492 of the Emirate of Granada, the last Spanish Islāmic state, Europe became almost completely Christian in faith.

By this time it also had a homogeneous and fully Christian art. Although that art had begun in an adaptation of Romano-Hellenistic forms, and was continually subject to minor influences drifting across from the Orient, and had on its fringes formed interesting syncretisms with Viking and Arabic art, and included much art of a secular kind, such as castles and love-lyrics—despite all this, it was by 1500 a thoroughly Christian art. Through many centuries it had been polished into a perfect instrument to serve the Christian cult and to express and teach the Christian faith, as these were understood in that age.

In contrast to Europe, the rest of the world was in 1500 at its nadir so far as Christianity was concerned. The hopeful 13th-century probings into Central Asia by the Franciscans, and their archepiscopal see at Zaitun in China, had long ago perished of neglect. The spectacular spread of Islām had reduced the Church in Asia to some pockets, mainly Nestorian, in the Levant, with an outlier in the little Church of the 'St Thomas Christians' in south-west India; in Africa, Christianity had practically shrunk to a weak 'Coptic' Church in Egypt and a semi-barbarian *enclave* in Ethiopia. The Crusades had long ago ceased, as failures; the more humane missionary efforts by St Francis of Assisi and Ramón Lull were also distant and had been ineffectual. It is true that the Iberian Powers had begun to stir: Ceuta was captured in 1415 and given a bishop in 1421; by 1490 a Portuguese advance down the west coast of Africa had reached the Kongo River and had even established a Christian realm there with a black king. But these were as yet only small and tentative gropings. Outside Europe Christianity hardly existed; and the arts outside Europe were non-Christian, or even in some ways anti-Christian, in the sense that they were as steeped in religion as was the Christian art of Europe, but had been formed in the expression of Faiths differing much from Christianity in dogma and in feeling.

Then, close to 1500, came the sudden end of Europe's self-containedness in territory and in religion. In 1492 Columbus had reached the Caribbean islands, and in 1498 had landed on continental America. In 1498 also the Portuguese had reached South India, and in 1510 they established their secure base at Goa. By the end of the 16th century Spain held most of Central and South America, with the Philippines, while Portugal ruled Brazil and also a chain of trading stations all round Africa and Asia to Macao. In the 17th, 18th and 19th centuries came similar expansions by more northerly and mainly Protestant Powers, notably Britain and Holland. By the end of the 19th century about three-quarters of the globe was either ruled from Europe or was under governments of European race and language. The 20th century is busy taking to pieces much of this European structure; but in some areas it is permanent, and in the others many of its effects endure.

Much of the motivation of this European expansion was economic and imperialistic; some of its methods were unchristian in the extreme. Yet it did involve a great expansion of Christianity. In the earlier phase, that of the Iberian Catholic Powers, this missionary purpose was constant and official. Under the *padroado* system the Pope had granted the two Catholic Powers exclusive territorial rights, and in return they accepted a missionary responsibility which they, on the whole, faithfully fulfilled, even after the *padraodo* system had come to show evangelistic weaknesses and was partially superseded. The Jesuits and the great Orders were at hand to provide the learned and sacrificial clerical manpower that was needed for effective mission. When the Protestant Powers came to trade and colonize abroad they were far less missionary-minded; officially they observed strict religious neutrality for the sake of political and commercial quiet; at times they even restricted their clergy to doing chaplaincy work for their fellow expatriates. But by the turn of the 18th and 19th centuries unofficial Protestant missionary societies had become very lively evangelistic forces, just when their Catholic counterparts were somewhat stagnating. In one way or another, then, about 1500 Christianity, after centuries of consolidation and relative quiescence within Europe, again became a missionary religion, and this time on a world-wide scale.

Where there is a Christian Church, there must be Christian art. Poverty or puritanism may at times reduce it to a minimum; but always there must be at least the implements and buildings for the cult. Much more, of course, is possible, and has often been desired and produced. Europe already had a rich heritage of such art; the new missionary Church needed quickly to acquire something equivalent.

Inevitably, such provision began in purely European modes. Small devotional objects and cult-implements were fairly easily imported from Europe: even the stone for whole churches was sometimes shipped as ballast from Portugal to Brazil! For the most part, however, missionaries took out design-books, and from them, and from memories of home, they did their best, often a very good best, as architects; and the cult-objects and ornaments were soon copied, cheaply and faithfully, by local craftsmen. All this was loyal to European styles; the expatriates—missionaries, officials, merchants and soldiers alike—could scarcely imagine, still less desire, any other kind of Christian art than this, which satisfied alike their natural nostalgia, their imperialistic superiority-complex, and their orthodoxy of belief. And these Western forms were accepted unquestioningly by the native converts, overawed as these were by the prestige of the conquerors. Indeed, the converts often came to be even more conservatively Western than the missionaries, because they were able to feel, more keenly than could the less involved newcomers, the pull of the non-Christian associations of the local arts.

Nevertheless, quite soon the opposite policy came to be advocated, that of the use of local art-forms for Christian purposes, the policy technically called 'adaptation' or 'indigenization'. The predominance of the expatriates lessened, and new nationalisms arose; then many came increasingly to feel that Western art, so satisfactory for the Church of the West, because there it was the art of the people, was for that very reason less than satisfactory for other lands and other peoples; it was involving Christianity in unnecessary association with foreignness, often even with oppression; and this came to be felt as a barrier to the understanding and acceptance of the Gospel. Apart from such theories, some measure of indigenization was often unavoidable, because of practical factors of climate, availability of materials, and the type of labour that had to be used.

Yet, much copying of the West has continued; and this has been not altogether because of pride or timidity in missionaries or nationals, but also for more valid reasons. In architecture, some local forms are simply not functional for Christian purposes; for instance, the liturgy practised in a Hindu temple, which is thought of as the house of a king-like god who receives offerings from and gives *darśana* to his worshippers as individuals or family groups, dictates a building-plan quite other than that which is required for a large Christian congregation gathered round the Word and Sacraments. Again, in figurative art, the sexual vigour of many Hindu representations of deities, and the impassive majesty of the great Buddha-figures, body forth aspects of God which to the Christian are true only if openly balanced by other aspects. Again, it has become usual nowadays in Africa to portray Christ as a negro: this makes the imaging of the Gospel easier for Africans, and has much theological justification in its thorough-going understanding of the Incarnation as 'Immanuel, God with us'; yet clearly it moves somewhat away from the Gospel as historical fact; and this may be thought a serious matter for a historical religion. In general, adaptation, being acceptance of local cultures, may make it hard for a local Church to fulfil its prophetic duty of bringing its own culture under the judgment of Christ. The Church in the West has failed often enough in this respect, without the Younger Churches repeating its errors.

The theoretical issues concerning adaptation being thus finely balanced, it is neither surprising nor improper that there has been much variation about it in practice. There has been much pure or nearly pure Europeanizing, an increasing amount of full indigenization, and, in between, many varieties of hybridization. Among the experiments in indigenization and hybridization, there have been many heavy, insipid compromises, much sound craftsmanship, and a few achievements of innovating genius.

Thus the Christian art of Asia and America after 1500 A.D. provides much material for studying, on a large scale of time and space, achievements and problems not only of missionary strategy, but of wide concerns in aesthetics and sociology. For a full study of such questions, account would have to be taken of Christian art beyond the limits of this fascicle—that of Europe in its Hellenistic and Celtic beginnings and in its northern area of the Vikings and in its southern Saracenic period, that of mediaeval Asia, and that of Africa. Useful comparisons would be sought, also, from parallel phenomena outside of Christianity—the chameleon-like adaptations of Jewish art, the diverse forms acquired by Islām throughout Asia and Africa, the blendings of Indian and Chinese traditions as

Hinduism and Buddhism spread over South-East Asia, and (more general still) the whole *corpora* of anthropologists' discussions of 'acculturation' and aestheticians' debates on the sociology of art. Even so, there are, within the limits of Asia and America after 1500 A.D., abundant materials for such study, and there are besides many interesting and beautiful artefacts simply to enjoy for their own sakes.

In the remaining Sections of this Introduction, a mental movement will be made round the globe from Europe eastwards. Nothing will be said, however, about what might have been expected to come first, the extreme western part of Asia, 'the Levant'. This is because, though the Christian arts of Syria and Armenia are of major importance, their main achievements antedate 1500, although some good work in the local styles has continued after that (Pl. I, 1). The first area to be considered, therefore, is Persia.

II. *Persia*

Persia, with boundaries roughly the same as those of the modern State of Īrān, has been, since the beginnings of Islām, solidly loyal to that Faith. Yet, lying as it did across what were till modern times the main trade-routes of the world, it has always been open to outside influences in art, though at first these came more from China than from Europe.

Persian painting of the classical period abounds in themes which would normally be called Christian, but which derive not from the Bible but from the *Qu'rān*. As the Patriarchs and Prophets of Israel, and also Mary and especially Jesus, are greatly honoured in Islām, they often appear in Persian pictures, but according to Islāmic traditions which frequently vary greatly from the Biblical accounts: thus, the Nativity is shown as taking place in a desert (Pl. I, 2); and a favourite subject is the lovely story of Jesus and the dead dog, which is in the *Ḥadīth* but in neither the Gospels nor the *Qu'ran* (Arnold 1928, 1965: chap. vi, 1932: chaps ii, iii).

There were, however, numerous direct artistic contacts with the Christian West, notably with the Portuguese. But nothing now remains of their great fort at Ormuz (1507-1622), or of their 17th-century mission churches at Iṣfahān; only, on the maritime approaches, there are the foundations of a star-shaped votive church of Our Lady of Victories built on Socotra in 1507 (Botting 1958, 1958) and at least one castle chapel, at Fort Mirani, Masqāṭ.

Exchanges of embassies brought some Christian art to Persia. A Papal embassy to Shāh 'Abbās I included several Christian art-objects among its presents; among them was a set of mediaeval Old Testament illustrations which greatly impressed the Emperor (Pl. II, 1; Cockerell 1927, 1969). Under Shāh 'Abbās II an embassy from Persia to Rome included the painter Muḥammad Zamān, who is said to have been baptized as a Christian in Rome and who certainly, on his return to Persia, then in India and then in Persia again, produced pictures which show much European technique, particularly in the landscape parts, and some are actually copies of Italian-Flemish Christian pictures (Pl. II, 2). Zamān is commonly regarded as one of the main introducers of the European elements which were prominent in Persian painting thereafter (but there is a Persian copy of a 'Virgin and Child and St John' which is dated 1640; and Iskander Munshī (1587-1629) says of Mawlānā Shaykh Muḥammad Shīrāzī that 'in Persia he was the man who imitated European models and made this style of painting fashionable').

More Christian art was brought to Shāh 'Abbās I's doorstep by the Armenians, who in 1606 were transported from Julfa on the north-western border to a specially-created suburb of Iṣfahān, New Julfa. There they built a set of fine churches in pure Persian style; but they filled them with European pictures acquired through their commercial contacts with Italy, and with imitations of such made locally (Pl. III, 1, 2; Carswell 1968); and they continued to work at their traditional type of manuscript illumination.

There were, besides, as was usual in those times in Western Asia, a number of wandering artists from Europe undertaking such commissions as they could contrive. Thus 'one John a Dutch-man (who had long served the King)'—actually he was a Flemish Jew—frescoed the pleasure-palace at Ashraf for Shāh 'Abbās I. Such work assisted Westernization, but not Christianity, since the subjects were usually either erotic or military. Sir Thomas Herbert, during his embassy of 1626/9, was much offended at the paintings in the Shāh's Farāḥabad palace of 'sundry representations of venereous gambolls, his Concubines studying by amorous postures to illure his favor ... such immodest postures of men and women, nay of Paederastyes, as makes the modest eye swell with shame'; he dwells on them in detail, even though they 'so much offended our eyes with shame, that they are in no wise fit to be remembered'. He also reports wall-paintings in the house of the Duke of Shīrāz, which were 'Trophies of his *Ormus* Victory, which is painted in Gold by a *Portugall* Captive' (Herbert; Carswell 1972).

Indeed, with rare exceptions, Christian art has had little appeal or production in Persia unless as a trifling with the exotic. The lovely Shīrīn, who appears so often in classical Persian painting, was a Christian Armenian princess, but she is shown only as a nubile beauty, naked or half-clad. Christian themes, especially the 'Madonna and Child', are not uncommon in 19th-century Qājār lacquer- and enamel-ware, but only in copies of the more sensuous late Italian works, or flippantly adorning toilet articles (Robinson 1969; Falk; Sotheby's and Christie's Catalogues).

In contrast with this, it is pleasant to see how, in the present century, in the numerically tiny Anglican Diocese of Iṣfahān, buildings and pictures have been commissioned which are models of what indigenized art should be (Pls IV, 1, 2) (Lehmann 1955; pl. 165; 1966, 1969: pl. 207).

III. *India*

In India—a term used here in its old sense, to cover the three modern States of India, Pakistan and Bangladesh—Christian art has had a long history. But the rather scanty remains of the pre-Portuguese art of the ancient 'Syrian' Church of Kērala (Pl. VI, 1), and the records of an early-14th-century church at Quilon built by a Dominican bishop and adorned a little later with paintings by a wandering Franciscan, fall outside our period, which begins almost exactly with the arrival, in 1498, of the Portuguese, in their dual search for 'Christians and spices'.

Under the strong missionary impulse of the newcomers, the west coast of India quickly received a chain of large churches in Portuguese Baroque which, despite the usual provincial coarsening of design and execution and flattening of ornament, would do credit to any small town in Portugal, and those in 'Golden Goa' would not disgrace Lisbon itself (Pls V, 1, 2) (Fonseca; Mártires Lopes; Chicó 1954, 1954, 1956; Azevedo 1954, 1956, 1959, 1970; Snead; Gune, 1965, 1965; Pereira, 1970, 1973). There were, besides, many smaller churches of the same type in other areas of India—around Āgra, in Bengāl and at Madras (Pl. VI, 1) (Hosten 1936).

A few exceptions should be noted to the 'Portuguese Baroque' style of this work. In the first place, it was not entirely Baroque. In the earliest building, there was a little Gothic—some true Gothic vaults at Goa and Madras (Pl. VI, 1), some false ones at Chaul (Mitterwallner), and a fine Manoeline doorway at São Francisco, Goa. By the late-18th-century, the Baroque of some churches faded into the more fragile elegance of the Rococo (Pl. VI, 2). Throughout, especially in the smaller churches, there is much that looks strangely like Romanesque (Pl. VII, 1). (The Romanesque tradition had never really died in Portugal, and there some of the finest Baroque interiors are gilt plaster decoration over Romesque architecture; perhaps, too, in India the expatriates preferred to recall the older style of their village churches rather than to ape the latest Lisbon fashion, and the simpler Romanesque forms would be more within the scope of their amateur architects and newly-trained local craftsmen.)

Further, it was not entirely Portuguese. Although the Portuguese authorities jealously guarded their *padroado* rights, and kept firm political control of the missions by reserving the highest posts for their own nationals and by routing the clergy through Lisbon, yet their man-power shortage was such that many missionaries of other nationalities were admitted, and these sometimes brought their own building-styles with them: a notable case is the very Italian Theatine church at Goa (Nossa Senhora da Divina Providência, 1656/61). In the Goa Territories there are even some examples of what looks very like Chinese influence, in Christian churches as well as Hindu temples (Pl. VII, 2). (There was considerable Chinese trading activity in the Indian ports, and at any rate in the 18th and 19th centuries many Chinese artists were working in British India.)

One would have expected to find a considerable measure of Indian influence; but in fact this is rare, in architecture and painting and fixed decorations along the West Coast. At Goa itself, the *Sé Patriarcal* (1562/1640) has a font and a stoup of Indian work, and its Capela de Santa Cruz dos Milagres has a screen of markedly Gujarātī style; it also has quite a picture-gallery, including an early cycle of the life of St Catherine, the patron saint of Goa's first church, for which pictures were originally imported from Europe. Several other of the major churches and convents have some oils and frescoes. The great nunnery of Sta Monica at Goa (1606/27) has an amazing set of frescoes, in which the features are much Indianized and the gospel personages are shown in the rather startling Portuguese dress of the time, much more so than they were in Portugal itself (Azevedo 1959). Also at Goa, the Priorado do Rosário (1543 on) has a font like that at the *Sé*, and also a memorial plaque to the widow of Governor de Sa (pre-1549) in a strange mixture of Renaissance and Gujarātī styles. At Damâo the *Sé* and the Madre de Deus Church have conch-decorations over the side-altars which seem influenced by Śrī Vishnu's cobra-hoods.

The lavish use of Christian art in the churches was not merely a social and aesthetic display; it is recorded as having had a considerable evangelistic effect. It is also recorded that humbler kinds of religious art, such as prints of the Crucifixion, were much sought after for use in the homes of the people. At first such things were imported from Europe, but soon they were being copied in Goa. But Christian art, in places under direct Portuguese rule, was protected from any dangerous kind of Indianization. The clergy, backed in the last resort by the Inquisition, created or at least supervised the architecture, and there was frequent legislation forbidding any kind of church art to be practised by non-Christians.

Further from Goa, there was rather more Indianization, even in architecture. The Jesuits' Padres Santos Chapel (1611), at the Old Āgra Cemetery, Lashkarpur, closely resembles a small Muslim tomb. The Holy Rosary Church, at Tejgaon, near Dacca, is in a charming Bengālī Baroque (Pl. VIII, 1). The great Roberto de Nobili, as a part of his complete self-Indianization at Madurai, built his chapels in Indian style: none of these now remain, though an 18th-century Jesuit told of a church then at Madurai in mixed Indian and European style.

In the 'minor arts' there was a good deal of Indianization, even in objects made for use in churches or at devotions. Much church silver, showing Indian traits, was produced for local use and also for export (Couto, 1928, 1956); *Art and the E.I. Trade*; *Arte nas Provincias*). The greatest creation of Goanese silverwork is the shrine at Goa containing the uncorrupt body of St Francis Xavier, the centre of vast pilgrimages. It is curious that this shrine, the greatest piece of all Indo-Lusitanian art, should be set in a marble mausoleum, sent out in 1698 by the Medici Grand Duke of Tuscany, which is the bulkiest artistic import from Europe. Smaller and humbler, yet artistically finer, is the bronze casket which once held the reputed bones of St Thomas the Apostle, at San Thomé Cathedral, Madras, which is built on the traditional site of his tomb: its decoration is more indigenized and also much more lively than the able but rather dead patterns of the Goanese work (Figredo).

There was never any export trade from India of indigenously-adorned ecclesiastical vestments, such as there was from China, though Goa itself does have some Mughal vestments as well as Persian and Chinese ones. But in the cheaper craft of cotton prints there are some Indian Christian representations (Pl. IX).

Two crafts developed in Goa, which became major trades and in which Indian and European elements were thoroughly mixed.

One was the profuse and high-quality manufacture of Indo-Portuguese furniture, European in shape but with Indian inlaid ornament, much of which was exported to Europe (Edwards and Codrington). Some, including most of the exports, was for secular use; but the churches in India had their share of it (Pl. VIII, 2), chiefly as the furnishings of the sacristies.

The other was the carving of ivories, mostly religious in subject and intended presumably for devotional use. Most of this work, though somewhat Indianized, is of unimpeachable orthodoxy (Pl. X, 1). There is, however, one common type among these ivories which is (to put it mildly) very odd iconographically. It shows Christ as the Good Shepherd, though somewhat plump and sleepy (Pl. X, 2). This seems based on a confusion between Christ and Kṛṣṇa, such as occurs elsewhere among Hindus of a syncretistic turn of mind, partly because of the similarity of names and ages. One can see here the reason for the flow of decrees at Goa against non-Christians doing work for churches! (By a curious coincidence, in the earliest phase of Christian art, at the catacombs, the Good Shepherd then also was a popular subject, and then also was modelled on pagan deities, Orpheus or Apollo or Hermes 'Criophoros'.)

Though it was so excellent, copious and widespread, this Portuguese art had strangely little influence in the South, where the proximity of Goa and the traditional tolerance of

Hinduism might have been expected to invite imitation. But apparently the only case of this is in the Italian-style secular paintings done for the Muslim Court of Bījāpūr, which is very close to Goa, at the Āthār Maḥall (mid-16th-century) and Kumatgī (mid-17th-century) (Cousens 92-94, 125 and pls. lxxv, lxxvi, cxi). A Jesuit Mission from San Thomé to the Chandragiri Emperor Venkata II in 1598/1600 used Christian pictures; but neither this, nor the gift made about 1680 by the Dutch Governor of Negapatam of a battle-scene, in an attempt to prove to a sceptical King of Golkundā that Europe did know the use of cavalry, had any effect, except a slight infiltration of Western feeling into some Deccanī painting.

In contrast to this, there was a great channel of Portuguese and Christian art-influence in India, through the Jesuit Mission to the Mughal Imperial Court, first at Lahore, and after 1601 at Āgra. This Mission, though it was an important diplomatic link for the Goa Government, and though its missionaries were till 1637 controlled by the *padroado* and routed through Lisbon and Goa and were interchangeable with the Goa personnel, nevertheless worked very independently. Its distance from Goa was considerable; its work lay in 'Mogur', at that time thought of as a different country from 'India', with languages quite different from those of the South (Persian for the nobles, Hindustānī for the common people); and very few Portuguese officials and merchants had any access to the Court. There the Jesuits were at the centre of a great Imperial Power, quite unlike the small warring kingdoms of the Deccan and the Coasts. So they used there an approach quite different from that in and around Goa, one which was akin to their technique in China and Japan—that is, direct dealing with the highest in the land, in learned and sympathetic cultural contact. (Blunt: 27-52; Smith 1911: 463-466; 1930: 216-217; 1962: 190-191; Hosten 1922; Clarke; Kühnel/Goetz 1924: 1-11, 38-58 and pls 29, 30, 40-43; 1926: 1-13, 46-68 and same pls; Stchoukine: 39-41, 45-50 and pls xixa, b, xxia, xxiva, c; Maclagan: esp. chaps xv and xvii; Jennes 1947, 1968; Camps; zu Löwenstein; Welch: 29-30 and pl. 14; Gascoigne; Butler 1972, 1973: chap. xiii; Beach; Devapriam.)

After a tentative visit by Fr Pereira in 1578, the first Mission came to the Court in 1580/3, under Bl. Rudolph Acquaviva, nephew of the Jesuit General himself (Pl. XI, 1); the second was in 1591; and thereafter there was a continuous presence from 1595 to 1803. In its earliest years it enjoyed great freedom of access to discussion with the Emperor himself and with his leading nobles (Pl. XI, 1); this privilege decreased somewhat after the death of Akbar in 1605, and drastically at the accession of Aurangzeb in 1658; but it did not entirely vanish till the death in 1803 of the last resident missionary, an *ex*-Jesuit by then, thirty years after the suppression of his Society.

Throughout, the Mission made great use of art, but not primarily of architecture as at Goa. It never had the numbers to need large churches, nor would such have been discrete, since at many times the Court and still more the populace were suspicious and even occasionally hostile. Churches were indeed built in the large Court towns, and in many scattered outstations, some even in Bhūtān and Tibet. Nothing now remains of them, except the Āgra cemetery chapel already mentioned, a chapel at Narwar, and perhaps some part of the 'Native Chapel' or 'Old Cathedral' at Āgra, which incorporates the 1636 chapel of the Fathers' residence, but only after later heavy repairs and enlargement.

The chief art used by the Āgra Jesuits was pictorial. Strangely, in view of the opposite policy of the Jesuits in China and Japan, they made very little use of artists of their own.

It is true that a painter named Domingo Pires, described a 'Portuguese' but also as an 'Armenian Christian', who was an interpreter as well, and who gave a good deal of trouble, was with Acquaviva's Mission in 1590; he then accompanied Jerome Xavier to Lahore and there copied a 'Madonna' for Prince Salīm (later the Emperor Jahāngīr); nothing further is heard of him. In 1626 an artist was assigned to the Āgra-based Tibet Mission, but he died before the expedition set out. (Likewise, in Goa and South India, there is evidence of the presence of a few, but only a few, Jesuit trained painters and architects.)

Occasionally the Fathers themselves commissioned Indian artists to make Christian paintings, for illustrating propaganda-texts presented to potentates. The copy of Jerome Xavier's Persian *Life of Christ* given to Akbar was illustrated by pictures made without European models but with oral instructions from the Fathers (Pl. XI, 2); the copy presented to Prince Salīm was illustrated later at the Prince's commissioning. When in 1607 they gave Jahāngīr a Persian *Lives of the Apostles*, this was 'interleaved with many pictures of their sufferings', some of which Jahāngīr had copied later in his Āgra palace frescoes. But for the most part the Fathers relied upon imports, of oils for their own churches and as presents to the very great, and of engravings as presents to both the great and the lesser.

The oils aroused special interest, the medium being novel to India. Some with secular, but most with religious, subjects were brought as presents to the Court; they were greatly appreciated there, and the religious ones were shown great reverence by Akbar and Jahāngīr themselves. The arrival and display of a copy of the Borghese Chapel 'Madonna' in 1580 attracted crowds of courtiers, artists and commonalty; Akbar himself visited the church to see it. There were similar scenes when a copy of the 'Madonna del Popolo' arrived in 1602, and an 'Adoration of the Magi' in 1608. Besides these show-pieces, the Fathers also used images in processions and in the very popular cribs.

The engravings were even more important, since in those days they provided the only cheap way in which pictures could be reproduced and transported. Even in Europe, they were the principal means whereby artistic influences spread; and missionaries all over the world were constantly writing home for more supplies of them, to be used as presents and propaganda, for domestic devotions and as models for artists. They were especially suitable in Islāmic countries, where the handling and discussion of small pictures in album collections formed an important part of culture.

The Fathers presented Christian engravings generously at the Court. Even the Emperor was glad to receive them; and we hear of Akbar personally selecting Christian items from his collection for his own artists to copy, and Jahāngīr likewise selected Christian engravings to be copied onto his palace walls, bidding his artists consult the Fathers as to the colouring. We know also that many of the Jesuits' religious discussions with both Akbar and Jahāngīr took place over the Christian pictures in the Emperors' albums.

Both these Emperors had many Christian pictures on the walls of their palaces; all these have now vanished, but we have accounts and even illustrations of them (Pl. XII). Jahāngīr went so far as to adorn the tomb of his father Akbar at Sikandra with Christian frescoes, which were later destroyed by the orthodox and puritanical Aurangzeb. William Hawkins reported from Āgra in 1609/11 that Jahāngīr was then saying his morning prayers before a picture of Christ and the Virgin engraved on stone.

However, much the main use of Christian engravings by Indian artists was in the production of album pictures. Hundreds of such, with Christian subjects, survive. In many cases the European prototype is known (Pls XIII, XIV), but often not as yet. Sometimes the Indian artist did no more than colour the actual engraving; more often he made as accurate a copy as he could, and then either left it as a drawing, or added colour according to his own ideas (*ibidem*). However accurately he was copying, minor Indianizations would creep in, through the features and backgrounds, and in the use of a more even line than in European drawing (*ibidem*). Often there are major indigenizations, notably the representations of the gospel personages in Indian and Portuguese dress; pictures of this kind seem often to be free compositions or *genre* studies rather than copies of any particular engraving (Pl. XV, 1). Even so, they generally preserve historical and iconographical orthodoxy, though there are occasional lapses into doctrinal errors (Pls XV, 2, XVI, 1, 2). Sometimes there are insensitivities, as when a 'Madonna' is made out of a prototype of a European society woman taking her siesta; and there is a whole series of pictures in which the Magdalen is confused with a well-known Muslim female penitent. There are oddities such as angels wearing only feather- or leaf-skirts, which are otherwise reserved for a few scenes from the *Rāmāyaṇa* and for pictures of hill-tribesmen—though they are also used once, very appropriately, for Adam and Eve at the Expulsion (Brit. Mus. Add. 18376, fol. 11 (1591): Stchoukine 1964: Pl. viii). And there are some atavistic Persianizings of Biblical personages. When pictures were taken from the central Court to provincial ones, and artists drifted away from the capital with Imperial patronage dried up, as under Aurangzeb, then provincial styles infiltrated into some of this Christian work.

In the more than two centuries of this very varied output, it is surprising to find only one or two examples of what can be thought to be anti-Christian feeling (Pl. XVII, 1). It is true that in many of the pictures of Christian subjects the features have been scratched out by a later hand; but this was generalized iconoclasm, directed not specifically against Christian representations, but impartially against Muslim ones as well.

Indeed, the high proportion of Christian themes in the *corpus* of Mughal miniatures is somewhat amazing. Though much of it was due to the intensive use of art by the Jesuit Mission, beginning in 1580 with Acquaviva's presentation to Akbar of a Polyglot Bible illustrated with Flemish pictures, it had other sources as well. Indeed, Christian pictures had reached the Court before the Jesuits: when Acquaviva arrived at the Sikandra palace in 1580, to his surprise he found pictures of Christ, Mary, Moses and Muḥammad in the Imperial dining-room, with Akbar paying reverence to that of Muḥammad less than to the others. Later, Christian pictures were among those brought as presents by Dutch and British embassies.

It is true that there were secular as well as Christian art influences at work in Mughal India. Free-lance European artists drifted over to the Court, as they had done for centuries to the Courts in Central Asia. Indeed, Manucci says that the original summons to the Jesuits was in order to get chaplains for the European artists, as well as soldiers, at the Court. The English embassy in 1583 included a jeweller and a painter, taken along because such were known to be welcome at the Court; the jeweller was taken into Akbar's service, though the painter had become a Jesuit at Goa because of imprisonment and poverty. There were two English artists at Jahāngīr's Court alongside the Jesuits; a mysterious Austin of Bordeaux is said to have been responsible for the inlays of the Peacock Throne at Delhi and for some work on the Tāj Mahal; Geronimo Veroneo was almost certainly associated with the *intaglio* work at the Tāj Mahal (though the tradition that he was the architect of the Tāj is nowadays almost universally rejected); at the Āgra cemetery is not only his tomb (1640), but also that of Manucci's friend Bronzoni (1677), 'a Venetian lapidary', whose tasks at the Court had ranged from cutting the Koh-i-Nūr diamond to building a ship for Aurangzeb. The gifts of Sir Thomas Roe's embassy of 1616/8 included oils of a 'Mars and Venus' and a 'Judgment of Paris', and a 'Diana' which was reported to have 'given great content'; a 'Venus and Satyr' was judged by Roe to be unsuitable, not as pagan or erotic, but as liable to racial misunderstandings! He did, however, also distribute some Christian pictures. The gifts of a Dutch embassy included battle scenes, comic pictures and nudes.

Yet these non-Christian themes attracted comparatively little copying or imitation at the Court studios. There was indeed some interest in copying European portraits; there were occasional *genre* pictures of Portuguese life, and even a few essays in the depiction of Indian subjects in Western style. But the pictures of Greek and Roman mythology were hardly ever copied, in spite of their erotic appeal; and Western landscapes were practically never imitated, except occasionally as backgrounds. There would seem to have been a deliberate preference for Christian subjects, not to be explained merely by the attraction of the exotic or by sporadic policies of syncretism at the Court. It might be *simpliste* to suppose that the Gospel was making its own appeal, aided only by adroit use of exotic subjects and technique. More sophisticatedly, Fr zu Löwenstein has suggested that the Indian artists were fired by the challenge of a task new to them, that of painting something beyond either mere mundane fact or mere imagined mythology— the truly historical Divine, the Transcendent shining through humanity, 'the Word made flesh'. Yet, did they ever really see this—or was it there to be seen in most of their prototypes?

Be that as it may, one can fairly claim that, in painting, Christian art made a real impact, at the Mughal Court, on the contemporary art of India. It was not the only Westernizing influence on that art, but it was the main one. It led not only to a spontaneous and copious production of pictures which combined Christian themes with Indian feeling, but also to a considerable change of Indian painting technique, in the general direction of realism, especially with perspective and *chiaroscuro*. This effect contrasts strikingly with the lack of influence by Portuguese architecture in India, which, though abundant and excellent, remained largely unindigenized and was not copied outside its own *enclaves*.

Overlapping with impacts by or through the Portuguese, came the major invasions of India by Western Powers, mostly Protestant. These brought in a multiplicity of Protestant Churches; the Christian art of this period in India was enlivened by a variety of national flavourings—British, French, Dutch, Danish—but with very little Indianization, except that in the French *enclaves* the Jesuits, though not some others of the Catholic clergy, permitted a good deal of near-Hinduism in the iconography of the popular paraliturgies (Norbert).

The official British church building, for the Indian Ecclesiastical Establishment (both Anglican and Presbyterian) was in fairly pure Western styles, often very fine, notably the Palladian of the oldest of all, St Mary's, Fort St George, Madras (1678/80), and of St George's Cathedral (1815) and St Andrew's Kirk (1818/21), Madras, and the 'Strawberry Hill' Gothic of St Paul's Cathedral, Calcutta (1784/7) (B. Clarke). Some of the more provincial specimens have a sort of official stolidity and betray the heavy hand of the military engineer acting as architect; nevertheless, the shaded openness required by the climate, and the use of an Indian speciality, 'egg-shell *chunām*' (a very hard and bright plaster), give the best of them a distinctive grace and charm. The unofficial churches used various Western styles with varying success.

For the churches of this period at the major centres much good monumental sculpture was imported from Britain. Thus, at Madras the Fort Church has three monuments by Flaxman and five by Bacon, and the Cathedral two by Chantrey and two by Flaxman; it was likewise at the other great Presidency and garrison centres. The richer Europeans often provided their dead with elaborate outdoor tombs, as in the Dutch cemetery at Pulicat and the old British ones at Calcutta. These were nearly always of local manufacture but in pure expatriate styles, though at Surāt there is a fine group of early-17th-century British tombs in an Anglo-Gujarātī style (Rawlinson). At the major mercantile centres an exotic note was provided by the gravestones of the Armenian communities, incised with the lovely national script.

In the later British period secular buildings showed more Indianization, ranging from the putting of a few oriental ornamental details onto heavy Western *pastiches*, to complete exercises in sundry Indian architectural styles (Nilsson; M. Archer 1968).

As for painting, a good many official oil portraits were imported, some by artists as distinguished as Ramsay, Hoppner and Lawrence. Several able Western professional painters worked in India—Tilly Kettle (1770/6), the great Zoffany himself (1783/9), Samuel and William Daniell (1784/94), Robert Home (1800/34, the last twenty of those years as Court Painter to the King of Oudh), George Chinnery (Madras and Calcutta, 1802/25, before he left for his better-known Chinese period (*George Chinnery*; Berry-Hill 1963, 1970). In the 19th century amateur artists abounded among the Europeans in India, even in the military (M. Archer 1972 *Conn.*). Little of this mass of work was on Christian themes or for church purposes, though the Fort Church, Madras, imported a 'School of Raphael' altarpiece, and the altarpiece at Calcutta Cathedral was both painted and presented by Zoffany.

This art by and for Westerners in India had considerable influence on contemporary art by and partly for Indians. In the graphic arts, the subjects were mainly secular. There was a vogue among the expatriates for *genre* pictures by Indian artists, in a style much affected by Western techniques and realism; this so-called 'Company art' was the pre-photographic equivalent of modern tourist postcards and snapshots (M. Archer 1947, 1969, 1972; W. G. Archer 1953; M. and W. G. Archer). (One special form of this memento art, that of painting on glass, is of odd interest, as having been brought to India by Chinese artists whose forebears in China had been taught the technique by 18th-century Jesuit missionaries (Appasamy)). Also, some zestful schools of Indian folk-painting at various centres, notably at Patna and Kālīghāt, did both secular and Hindu work in hybrid styles of a very similar nature (M. Archer 1947; W. G. Archer 1971).

Architecturally, Western influence came in this period to affect much Indian secular work, both domestic and official, and occasionally even Hindu temples (Pls XVII, 2, XVIII, 1). The buildings of the Hindu reforming sects and organizations, such as the Ārya Samāj and the Rāmakrishṇa Mission, owe much of their general design, as distinct from their ornamentation, to Christian churches (though there are also parallels in Buddhist halls), since their worship is of a congregational type in some ways more akin to Christian liturgies than to the individualistic *pūjā* of Hindu temples.

With the 20th century there came a reaction from Westernization. Already in 1896 E. B. Havell had come as Principal to the Calcutta School of Art, and had there begun not only his own teaching, which turned Indian art education back to Indian models, but also his inspiration of Abanindranāth Tagore, which later led to the Indian art centre of Śāntiniketan (W. G. Archer 1959). In this movement the Christian Church can claim to have done a little pioneering. From 1857 to 1887 at Lahore a Muslim tomb (actually that of one of Jahāngīr's favourite concubines!) was used as the Church of St James; and at Peshāwār in 1883 All Saints' Church was built in pure mosque style (Lehmann 1955: pl. 88). But these experiments were so isolated as to be almost eccentricities.

After the First World War, however, Indian Christian art began a real movement towards indigenization.

In architecture (Lehmann 1955: pls 84-87, 91-93; 1965, 1969: pls 193-200) there were, for Protestants, the famous experiments at Tirupattur (Pl. XVIII, 2) and Dornakal (Pl. XIX, 1) and many less well-known places (Pl. XIX, 2) (Hargreaves). The corresponding Catholic work was inspired by Costantini's initiative in China (Pl. XX) (Costantini: II, iv; *Indian Culture*; *Apostolic Approach*).

In painting, perhaps the principal pioneer was A. D. Thomas, well-publicized and greatly esteemed in the West; but some critics have felt that his Tagorean style of sensuous softness relates him more to Buddhism and Hinduism at their weakest than to the virile realism of the Gospel (Pl. XXI, 1). Frank Wesley, Angelo da Fonseca and many others have worked in a variety of styles, of which perhaps the Tagorean and the folk-art have been the favourites, though semi-abstractism from the West and neo-Mughalism have also been used (Pls XXI, 2; XXII, 1; XXIII, 1, 2) (S.P.G.; Costantini: II, iv; Lehmann 1955: pls 1, 2, 4, 5, 14, 15, 24, 25, 34, 35, 53, 54, 59-83, 89-90, 95-100, 109, 110, 119, 120, 137, 138; 1966, 1969: pls 142-192; Mazumdar; Lederle; James; Taylor; Takenaka). Despite an increasing number of church commissions, and the steady market for Christmas cards, this work suffers from lack of patronage. It is rightly publicized and praised for its Christian and aesthetic competence, but is at a stage of interesting experiments rather than of sustained mastery; it still lacks genius. How sad that the Catholic Church, which nurtured his boyhood, could not hold F. N. Souza, but lost him to the rival Western religion of Communism; his work has a dynamism which the Christian work misses (Mullins).

Perhaps the most hopeful of the experiments is in the work of Jyoti Sahi, who is seeking, across a semi-abstract Western technique, to practise an aesthetic based on the *śilpa-śāstras*, whereby art is more a sacrament working through the correct forms and formulae than the personal expression of 'beauty' or an ego (Pl. XXII, 2) (*Missionskalender*; Hargreaves; Taylor: 143-153; Jyoti Sahi). It is early yet to judge whether such an approach will succeed; if it does, then this is a kind of indigenization which goes much deeper into the Indian tradition and psychology than can any mere copying of 'styles'.

There have recently been attempts in the Indian Church at using—as the Jesuits had done in earlier days—the great and ancient Indian art of the dance as a means of presenting the Gospel story (Pl. XXIV) (Edmond; Lehmann 1966: 59-62; 1969: 57-61; Film). In this, there is no difficulty as regards the music: Indian music has long been used by the Church both in congregational praise and in paraliturgical Gospel narratives. Nor is there any difficulty, as there would be in the West, about undue secular associations. On the contrary, the difficulty is with religious associations, since the classical Indian dance is composed of stylized and symbolic gestures which are very closely linked with representations of Hindu mythology.

IV. *South-East Asia*

The great tract of mainland and island territory which lies between India and China and is partly unified by racial kinship, by a common adherence to Buddhism (though with a strong Muslim element in parts) and by similar though richly diversified types of art in which Indian and Chinese elements blend, was evangelized quite early in our period, but retains very little Christian art from the early times. The area was of prime importance to the first European adventurers, who were in search of the 'spice islands' rather than of India, and much missionary work was truly heroic, as that by Alexander of Rhodes (in Asia 1603/45). But missions to Buddhists and Muslims find it hard to put down roots; there was a lack of major metropolitan centres, with their special opportunities, such as India had in Āgra and Goa and China in Peking; and in Indonesia the Dutch ascendancy systematically destroyed Portuguese work and itself produced little that was outstanding. In 1965 Malacca had, as relics of its early Christian days, only a roofless and ruined Portuguese church, a Dutch church then used by the Anglicans, and a fine set of Portuguese, Dutch and Armenian tombstones. Scattered through the islands there also survive from the Portuguese period a few devotional ivories, statuettes and silver vessels in the possession of confraternities and individuals, and some tombstones, two church bells, one font, and a number of remarkable festival songs in a weirdly corrupted Portuguese *patois* (Bland; Pinto da França). Some influence in a strange 18th-century Javanese Muslim manuscript now at Manchester (Pl. XXV, 1), a charming little Burmese 'crib' in London (Pl. XXVI, 1), and, if they have survived recent wars, the amazing 'Père Six' churches in Annam (Pl. XXV, 2) — these would seem to complete the list of the old work still extant.

Throughout this area, including Sri Lanka (Ceylon), the modern Church has promoted many experiments in indigenized painting, sculpture and architecture (Costantini: II, iii, v; Lehmann 1955: pls 153, 154; 1966, 1969: pls 97-104, 202-206, 233-235). In Indo-China, the pioneer in this was C. Lé-Van-Dé, who was competent but derivative; work much more charming and also more indigenous has since been done in Indonesia by Wajan Tūrān and others; and S. Sudjojono and others have used modern Western idiom with dramatic effect. Archbishop Albert Sugijapranata, S.J., has experimented with Christian adaptations of the traditional Javanese 'shadow-plays' (Pl. XXVI, 2) (Lehmann 1955: pls 157, 158; Mylius).

V. *China*

Like India, China had strong Nestorian missions both early and mediaeval, and also a mediaeval interlude of Franciscan work from Rome. Indeed, both these types of mission were much stronger in China than in India; but both had come to a complete end by the middle of the 14th century. The only art-remains of this early Chinese Christianity are the famous 'Nestorian Stone' of Sian-fu, a collection of nearly a thousand Nestorian crosses and similar objects at the University of Hong Kong, and a set of mediaeval tombs recovered from the city walls of Zaitun, in origin Nestorian, Manichaean and Catholic, with a fine synthesis of Persian, Italian and Chinese motifs.

Two centuries later, an entirely fresh start was made when, in 1514 or 1515, the Portuguese first contacted China, and began trade with it through Macao. They acquired this town, under vague legal terms, in 1557, and continue to hold it—still rather ambiguously—today. Various religious Orders soon arrived, building bases in Macao and occasionally evangelizing in the hinterland; and it became a bishopric in 1575.

In four ways, Macao was an important centre for the cultural contact of Asia and Europe (Montalto de Jesus; Boxer 1942, 1948, 1959, 1968; da Silva Rego; Hugo-Brunt). In the first place, it was the port of entry and the base for the Peking Mission. Secondly it had, and retains, an architectural achievement of its own, with good Baroque buildings —the great Jesuit Church of São Paulo (1601/40; but the *façade* alone survived a fire in 1835), the Church of St Augustine (*c.* 1590/1620), the Church of St Dominic (16th and 17th centuries), and the Jesuit seminary and Church of St Joseph (1742/58). Thirdly, it had an export trade to Europe and elsewhere of Chinese-style vestments and ivories, not unlike the Goanese commerce in church furniture and silver and devotional ivories (Pl. XXVII, 1) (Ferrão). This trade continued for a long time; in the early 18th century Mexico Cathedral imported its great screen from Macao, and in 1810/1 Raffles, then at Malacca, employed 'a Chinese Macao painter who was good at painting fruit and flowers to the life'. Fourthly, it was for a time the artistic base of the Japan Mission, with a school for the training of Japanese Christian artists. (Actually the carving on the São Paulo *façade* is by Japanese craftsmen, betrayed as such by their bad Chinese script; and Macao still preserves some early oils of the Japanese martyrdoms.)

Macao, however, has been greatly overshadowed in Christian history by the fame of the Jesuit Peking Mission (Bernard 1935; Schüller 1936; 1940: 7-82; D'Elia; Costantini: 206-212; Rowbotham; McCall; Gallagher; Cronin; Cummins; Dunne; Loehr; Franke; Dehergne; Sullivan 1967: 212-217, 225-229; 1973: 47-86). In 1579 the great Jesuit organizer in Asia, Alessandro Valignano, and the even greater Matteo Ricci, arrived at Macao. In 1601 Ricci was able to reach and settle at the Court of Peking itself. There he and his successors, notably Adam Schall (in China 1619/1666), attained considerable prestige, symbolized by high mandarin rank (Pl. XXVII, 2). The basis of this was largely their expertness in astronomy—the Emperor's standing depended on his performance of the correct rites with accurate timing; the Chinese calendar had gone too far astray for the local experts to be able to correct it; but the Jesuits were able to set these vital matters right and to keep them so. In addition, they made skilful use of the novelty-appeal of European art, partly imported for presents at Court and for use in their own churches, but mainly produced locally by their own staff; this had included artists almost from the beginning, the half-Japanese Ni Yi-ch'êng (Niva) having joined Ricci at Peking in 1602. By such use of Western science and art, together with a brilliant and heroically sustained policy of indigenization in worship and manner of life, and by much personal bravery in times of xenophobia, the Jesuits contrived to keep a small but at times very influential Mission active at the Court, and through it generally secured some measure of protection for other missions of a more normal type elsewhere in China. The Mission lasted for over two centuries (Ripa; Bernard 1943); it survived, though much weakened, the dissensions of the famous 'Chinese Rites' controversy to which its extremes of indigenizations had led, and even the dissolution of the Society in 1773 (in China, 1775), its last member dying at Pekin in 1814 (as an *ex*-Jesuit then, of course).

This continuous artistic presence of Jesuits at the Chinese Court exercised considerable influence, in three spheres.

In the first place, several of them had to work almost exclusively in the palace studios on paintings ordered by the Emperor. These pictures had scarcely any Christian content or direct Christian influence, since the Emperors, even when they were men of culture and not under xenophobic pressure, were peremptory taskmasters, insisting on getting what they themselves wanted and nothing else (Attiret: 46-48). The only Court Jesuit who can rank as an artist of real eminence was Br Giuseppe Castiglione (1688-1766; at Peking 1715-66). He has left only two doubtfully-ascribed Christian paintings from his copious half-century's work in China; his special reputation was as a painter of horses (C. & M. Beurdeley 1971; Picard). (It is strange that he, who was held in special respect for his gentle saintliness, rose to much greater artistic power in this secular work in an alien medium than he had done in the apparently more congenial form of the Baroque religious oils of his earlier days in Italy and Portugal.) However, this Court work, though not of great Christian influence, had a more general importance, as being the main means whereby Western techniques of perspective and *chiaroscuro* entered Chinese painting— though the extent and source of this influence is much disputed among the experts (Sickman/Soper; Cahill/Sullivan; Sullivan 1973: 47-89).

Some of the Peking Jesuit artists, such as Niva, were sufficiently free from Court demands to be able to do Christian painting for the Mission's churches in and around Peking. This work was another channel of both Western and Christian influence: unfortunately very little of it survives (Costantini: 215-217; Lehmann 1955: pl. 102), though there was a painting by Niva at Ricci's tomb down to the Boxer Rebellion. In 1606 a noted Chinese *littérateur* included in his album-book copies of four Christian engravings given to him by Ricci, along with explanatory texts (Pl. XXVIII).

The second area of influence by the Jesuit Court artists was architecture. Not unnaturally, in view of their pre-eminence as astronomers, Jesuits built the Peking Observatory (1673). Rather less appropriately, Castiglione and his colleagues were called upon to design a group of pleasure-buildings in the Yuan-ming-yuan, the Summer Palaces (1747/59), which were world-famous till their wanton ruining by European forces in 1860 (Sirén; Adam). In each case Chinese decoration was put upon structures basically of European design. Unlike the paintings, these buildings, despite their fame, had no influence on Chinese architecture. The only Christian structures of this period still surviving seem to be some fragments of Ricci's tomb, which had been ordered by the Emperor himself (Planchet; Bernard 1934), and perhaps a 1640 church at Shanghai in full Chinese style. In their other churches, now destroyed, the Jesuit architects had hesitated, being aware of the dangers involved in too close imitation of temples, and had used either a European style or a mixed one like that of the Summer Palaces.

The third area of Jesuit influence through their Court connections was at the Imperial porcelain works. In the great mass of 'export china' which poured out from these both to Europe and to Asia there is a surprisingly high proportion of pieces decorated with Christian themes (Jourdain/Jenyns; Phillips; C. & M. Beurdeley 1974; M. Beurdeley; Lunsingh Scheurleer: 142-143, 151, 160-163, 169, 180 and pls 234-240, 300, 340). These used to be called 'Jesuit china', because the presence and influence of some Jesuit artists at the Imperial works is known from documentary evidence, and it was assumed that the Christian themes would have originated from them. But the term has been discarded nowadays, since it has become clear that the designs of the export porcelain had a multiplicity of European sources, many of them certainly non-Jesuit, even for the religious pieces. The great mass of armorial table-services, and similar sets with nautical designs, commissioned, with the help of engravings and wooden models, through factors ('*chine de commande*'), or by sea-captains on the China run; some, with pictures of brothel scenes or of 'Wilkes for Liberty', or with portraits of Calvin or Luther or even John Buckholdt of Leyden, 'King of the Anabaptists', certainly cannot have been made at Jesuit direction. Moreover, even when the pictures are orthodoxly Christian in subject, their spirit is often markedly unchristian (Pls XXIX, XXX).

Nevertheless, the Jesuits may well have supplied the prints for most of the Christian designs, and perhaps also for those with Classical themes, as we know that their Peking library contained books of such. And there were certainly Jesuits at the porcelain works, with enough influence to introduce some new techniques—indeed, throughout the centuries we hear of only two non-Jesuit foreign artists at work in or around Peking. There is even some evidence that they arranged for the surreptitious export of some Christian porcelain to the Church in Japan, otherwise quite isolated in its persecution (*cf.* Explanation to Pl. XXIX, 1).

In any case, however, one must always recall that the Chinese thought of their export ware as a thing apart, for foreigners; porcelain for home use was quite untouched by any Western influence in design.

In all this, the Jesuits played an ambiguously dual role. They were a Westernizing influence on Chinese art in general; but in their own church art they were pioneers of indigenization, in line with the general style of their mandarin lives and costly insistence on the 'Chinese Rites'.

In the 19th and early 20th centuries China, being for a while fully open to varied missionary activity and other Western contacts, suffered its share of the world-wide flood of dull Westernizings, in both Christian and secular art. There were, however, some mock flirtations with the local style of architecture, mainly by way of putting upswept eaves on top of otherwise Western buildings; and there were a few isolated experiments in full indigenization.

A sudden change from this came, at first in the Catholic Missions, shortly after Archbishop (afterwards Cardinal) Celso Costantini arrived in China as Apostolic Delegate in 1922. Trained as an artist before his ordination, Costantini was deeply aware of the importance of art in determining men's attitudes to the Christian Faith; and he was determined upon a radical polity of indigenization, in the artistic as well as other aspects of mission activity. His opportunity came early in 1923, when two Prefects Apostolic sent him routine information of their intention to erect several new churches. In reply, the doubtless astonished prelates received, instead of a formal comment, a longish essay on the history and principles of adaptation and the urgent need for it in China (Costantini 1949: 212-29). This tractate was published in several languages, as the basis for a long campaign whose climax was the Vatican Exhibition of Missionary Art, planned for 1940, but postponed, because of the War, till 1950.

Meanwhile in Peking the Apostolic Delegate had chosen, in 1929, an able non-Christian painter, Ch'en Yüan Tu, to execute a whole set of Christian pictures. In 1932 this artist requested baptism; then, as Luke Ch'en, he formed a group of artists, who were converts like himself, into the Art Academy at the Catholic University of Peking. This Academy's work, aided by adroit publicity, has enjoyed a considerable *succès d'estime* in the West; it is undoubtedly good and Christian, but some critics have felt that it is too solid and heavy to reflect the true Chinese spirit of light and grace (Pls XXXI, 1, 2) (Costantini: II, i; Schüller 1940: 83-147; Bornemann). He brought out a Dutch Benedictine, Dom Adelbert Gresnigt, to design buildings in Chinese style; this was done competently, but with far too heavy a hand. Similar work has been done elsewhere (Lehmann 1955: pls 101, 103-108, 111-118, 121-126, 155, 156, 173, 174; Shek-kai-nung/Skinsnes; Wang; Lehmann 1966, 1969: pls 105-133; Takenaka 1975)—at its best when it follows the peasant rather than the mandarin mentality (Pl. XXXII, 1).

One cannot find out how all this has fared in mainland China after the Revolution. However, in Taiwan (Formosa), where the Catholic Mission continues and flourishes, some fine work has been done in the erection of churches which combine honest and simple use of ferro-concrete techniques with a graceful Chinese spirit (Pl. XXXII, 2). At Hong Kong, a few Chinese Christian painters continue work, some of which is published as Christmas cards.

VI. *Japan*

The Church in Japan has suffered persecutions of such exceptional ferocity and persistence that much of its art has been both inspired and overshadowed by martyrdom.

Japan was for Europe at the end of a very long and difficult line of communication, and so Christianity reached it late. The first Portuguese arrived only in 1543. The first missionary was St Francis Xavier himself, landing in 1549. He stayed for two years, and learnt something of the language; but his real objective was always China, and in 1552 he died on an island just off the Chinese coast.

Other Jesuits soon followed, using their customary strategy of contacting the highest in the land. They established a presence at the Imperial Court itself, and often had some influence there, being the normal channels for commercial diplomacy. Japan was not yet encased in the almost psychotic self-sufficiency insisted on in the next century; but strong suspicion of foreigners was always only just below the surface. Portuguese commerce was restricted to one '*náo*', 'great ship', from Macao each year.

Nevertheless the Fathers did get on friendly terms with several of the great nobles, the semi-independent *daimyos*, and converted some of them; doubtless there was an affinity felt between the Jesuit and the *samurai* heroic outlooks on life. On this basis they founded a strong Church, said to number 300,000 souls by 1600. An embassy from the major Christian *daimyos* visited Rome between 1582 and 1590, and for a few years Nagasaki was actually an *enclave* under Jesuit rule.

This friendship with the leading *daimyos*, however, proved double-edged, as the central government was in this period struggling for authority over the turbulent feudal clanchiefs. Furthermore, the missionary monopoly of the Jesuits, those masters of diplomacy, was being broken by an infiltration of other Orders from Spanish Manila; these used less tactful methods of evangelization and aroused suspicions of European aggression. Even in 1597 twenty-six missionaries and converts had been crucified at Nagasaki, in 1614 a series of fierce general persecutions began; in 1638 all missionaries were banished; between then and 1643 all the missionaries who remained, and thousands of their converts, were relentlessly hunted down; one or two missionaries who entered surreptitiously after that were quickly caught and killed. Indeed, no foreigners were allowed on the mainland at all; the Dutch merchants, who had replaced the Portuguese as the foreign trade monopolists, were confined to Deshima, an island in Nagasaki harbour.

The persecutions were mild in one sense; the accused had only to signalize their renunciation of the Faith by treading on a sacred image (*fumi-e*) to be free of all penalty. But those who did not thus apostatize suffered appallingly. Besides crucifixions and burnings at the stake, there were more refined tortures, as by scalding with water from boiling hot-springs, or the prolonged agony of 'the pit'. For this, the victim was hung upside-down by the feet, with the head in a pit of ordure, and was kept conscious by light slashings of the brow; relief could be obtained at any time by signalling apostasy with a movement of a hand left free for that purpose. In 1632 the Jesuit Vice-Provincial, Cristovão Ferreira, caused great scandal by apostasizing after six hours in the pit (Endo). One young Japanese woman endured fourteen days of it before she died.

Amazingly, in spite of such horrors, several groups of crypto-Christians began to reveal themselves when missionaries returned to Japan in 1865. Without priests, and in constant danger of denunciation and death by torment, they had somehow retained some elements of Christian faith and practice. Even in 1955 30,000 of their descendents were still insisting on keeping up a quasi-Christian church life in the islands west of Kyushu, quite independent of the official Church.

During their 'Christian century', the Jesuits founded and fostered a partially indigenous Christian art. The contemporary non-Christian artists of the '*namban*' ('southern barbarian') screens, always exact in recording the European phenomena whose exoticism attracted them, show the Jesuits themselves in neat European clerical dress, but with churches built in fully Japanese style, except for the crosses surmounting them. Under the leadership of the great Valignano, the Mission imported many European pictures, but the local demand was for more. So, Japanese artists were trained, at first in Macao; then from 1603 to 1614 Giovanni Niccolò headed an art academy in Japan itself. The trainees began by copying European models, but soon they developed an increasingly Japanese style. Among them, Nobukaka achieved considerable fame, and stayed on during the persecutions.

Since these persecutions came to overshadow the whole life of the Church, they became determinative of its art. In Japan, Macao and Rome, several contemporary oil-paintings of the main martyrdoms survive. There still exists the banner, painted with an 'Adoration of the Blessed Sacrament', under which in 1637/8 the Christian *samurais* made their last desperate stand at Shimbara Fort in Kyushu. The most pathetic relics of those days are the *fumi-es*, bas-reliefs of Christ or the Virgin, with their higher parts worn smooth by the feet of those who signified apostasy by trampling on them. There are statuettes which to inspecting police would appear to be of Kannon, the God or Goddess of Mercy, but which have a small cross at the neck to make a Madonna, or have a Christian symbol incised on the back (Pl. XXXIII, 2); there are even crosses bearing a figure of Christ made like the Buddha (Pl. XXXIV, 1); some tea-bowls survive, marked with crosses, presumably for a secret liturgical or devotional purpose. In Bungo and Okago there are also cave-chapels which seem to belong to this period: the Church literally went underground! (Otsuki; Paske-Smith; Schurhammer; Shinmura; McCall; Costantini: 237-239; Nishimura; Grunne; Okamoto; Janeira; Kaga; Jennes; Sullivan: 14-19; Sakamoto/Yoshimura.)

It should be borne in mind that the church art of old-time Japan was only one facet of a general fascination with the West and its art. Even during the early persecutions there was a craze among the Japanese young bloods and their women for '*namban*' religious objects like crucifixes and rosaries as personal adornments. Iberian imports had some influence on Japanese ceramics. The theme of the arrival of the annual Portuguese *não* attracted some of the greatest masters of screen-painting, but their depiction of the Jesuits and the churches was merely as part of the exotic scene, without any religious interest. Later, when the only Europeans in Japan were the few Dutch in their Deshima confinement, and even mention of foreign religions was rigorously prohibited, there was a vogue for the *nagasaki-e genre* scenes of Chinese and Dutch foreigners (*c.* 1750 - *c.* 1860), and the *ukiyoe* perspective painting; and at the very end of the isolation came the 'Perry prints', 'Red-Hair prints' and *kaikwa-ban* ('civilization prints'). Some of this work was, like the Indian 'Company art', made for foreign purchase, but much of it reflected a yearning for experience of things outside Japan; it was in different ways and degrees Westernized, but was quite unconcerned with Christianity (Boxer 1936, 1950, 1958; Keene; Sullivan 1973: 20-45).

Since the reopening of Japan to the West, and then the revival of Christian missions followed by the development of indigenous Churches, much good Japanese Christian art has again been created, in buildings, paintings and other forms. In the paintings, the theme of martyrdom has remained common, rightly recalling the heroic history of the Japanese Church, and also according with the *samurai* traits which may be permanent in the national psychology (Pl. XXXIII, 1) (Costantini: 239-248; Straelen; Lehmann 1955: pls 127-134; 1966, 1969, pls 208-232; Yanagi; Takenaka 1966, 1975).

VII. *The Philippines*

At the Philippines, we leave the area of Portuguese influence for that of the Spanish. Although the archipelago was discovered by the Portuguese Magellan in 1521, the Spanish took control of it some forty years later, and held it for three centuries. When the see of Manila was founded in 1579 it was suffragan to Mexico. So the Philippines, along with their little associate Guam, have an art which is not Portuguese, arriving *via* Lisbon and Goa, but Spanish, linked with Seville through Havana and Acapulco.

Despite exceptional ravages of climate, fire, earthquake and war, they are full of magnificent old churches, in that rather heavy variant of Spanish Colonial style known as 'earthquake Baroque' (Pl. XXXIV, 2). Occasionally non-European elements appear in them. One church has a fine bas-relief of Indonesian style in the gable of its *façade*. The bell-towers often look very like Chinese pagodas, and certainly their builders were generally Chinese, but the insetting of the successive storeys of the towers may be merely a part of the precautions against earthquakes (Díaz-Trechuelo: p. xviii). Some of the decorations are clearly by Chinese craftsmen, and it is known that between 1581 and 1586 a Jesuit Father ran a school for Chinese painters who supplied the churches of

Manila with pictures based on Western models; also vestments were made locally. Some of this Sino-Filipino work was for export, especially the ivory carvings; and in the last quarter of the 18th century a Filipino sculptor was active in Argentina.

In the Philippines as elsewhere there is now a ferment of modern experiment in all the forms of Christian art (Takenaka).

VIII. *Oceania*

The small islands scattered over the Pacific were for the most part not evangelized till the 19th century; thereby they became subjected more than most mission areas to the horrors of the cheapest and poorest import art.

Nevertheless, there have been occasional daring adaptations, as with the font at Bau made out of the local cannabalistic killing-stone (Pls XXXV, 1, 2) (Tippett), the use of children's interpretation of Bible scenes in New Guinea forms at one new church (Pl. XXXVI, 1) (*Missionskalender*), and of ancestor-figures in the pillars of another (Pl. XXXVI, 2) (Costantini: II, x; Lehmann 1955: pls 140-148, 151; 1966, 1969: pls 237-282). Not infrequently the graceful and ornate forms of the local houses have been used in church architecture (though grave errors in symbolism have sometimes marred the effect of the indigenous decorations) (Lehmann 1955: pls 149-150).

The Pacific area has indeed had more than its fair share of comedies of unwise adaptation. An early and specially ludicrous example is—or was—Pomare's 'Royal Mission Chapel' at Papaoa, Tahiti. In 1819 King Pomare, a particularly headstrong man and then in the first flush of a convert's enthusiasm, insisted, against missionary advice, on building a church in Tahitian style, 54 feet broad and no less than 712 feet long. Thirty-six bread-fruit tree-trunks supported the roof along the centre. There was a stream flowing slantwise across the floor; its course had not been noticed when the building was begun, and its diversion would have been too laborious; so it was simply left to flow, with entrance and exit gratings in the walls. There were 133 windows and 29 doors. The royal optimism about the size was partly justified by a congregation estimated at between 5000 and 7000 at the opening service. This was an extraordinary affair, with three missionaries preaching simultaneously from three pulpits 260 feet apart, from three different texts. (One of these—Luke 14:22, 'And yet there is room'—would seem to have been singularly appropriate.) The hymns were synchronized from the central pulpit by a fourth minister, described as having 'a very shrill, penetrating voice'. Alas, two-and-a-half years later the king died of alcoholism and worse excesses; it is as well that his chapel did not long survive him (Cousins; Lovett; Haldane).

In modern times, the Pacific area has been the field of the eccentric religious phenomena called 'cargo cults'. These mingle elements from Christianity and other elements from local traditions with a materialistic fantasy of coming riches; this seems based on frustration at continued economic inferiority and reaction against Christian missions for not helping much in such matters (*Pacific Islands Monthly*; Worsley; Lawrence; Ashe). The movement has achieved its own art in sundry forms (Pl. XXXVI, 3), including even a church made in the shape of the aeroplane which is expected to bring the 'cargo'.

Australia and New Zealand, being inhabited mainly by European immigrants, are naturally full of Christian buildings, duly decorated, all in imitations of European styles, apart from a little aboriginal and Maori church art, rather self-consciously cultivated, and occasional more spontaneous syncretisms. (Lehmann 1955: pl. 139). In the history of the earliest of this European work there is a curious episode of appeals made for advice from the Camden Society in the 1840's; the Society invariably urged the use of Gothic, except that on one occasion in 1843 it acquiesced in the insistence of a patron in New Zealand that his church should be Norman, because this style, being 'rude', 'massive' and with 'grotesque sculpture' was more within the capacities and understanding of his Maori workmen (Germann)!

In contrast to this, little Hawaii—politically American, geographically Pacific, racially a melting-pot—has in its cultural turmoil achieved a few buildings in strikingly successful hybrid styles (Pl. XXXVII, 1, 2) (Lehmann 1955: pl. 168; Neil).

IX. *America*

If we do not count as American the deliberate imports of European mediaeval art—sometimes entire buildings—to modern museums, and the Gothic of the earliest churches in the islands of the eastern Atlantic and the foundations of a 13th-century cathedral (marvellously adapted to local materials and climate) in Greenland, then all the art of the Americas falls within our period. Columbus 'discovered' some of the offshore islands as early as 1492, and reached the mainland in 1498; but the decisive European penetrations came more than twenty years after that.

Once established, the Iberian towns in America, fabulously wealthy through loot, cheap labour and the mines of gold, silver, mercury and gems, were during the next three centuries filled with large churches, whose simple but sound design, combined with lavish ornament instinct with pioneering vitality (Pls XXXVIII, 1-2), produced what some would hold to be the finest of all the local variants of Baroque. Even the humble rustic shrines of adobe and straw in peasant villages show much of the same inner nobility, like decayed *hidalgos*, shabby Don Quixotes (Pl. XXXIX, 1).

The basis of the style of these great churches is Iberian Baroque, in spirit and in decoration, if not in the handling of space, with its by-forms of Rococo and Churrigueresque—this last was exceptionally congenial, and reached its fullest development in America. But there were major variations.

First, the American work was often archaistic. Some of the early churches, notably at Santo Domingo in Hispaniola and at Puerto Rico, were completely in Gothic; and later, even till near the end of the 17th century, churches basically Baroque were roofed with elaborate Gothic vaults (Pl. XXXIX, 2). *Mudéjar* ceilings were likewise long in favour, partly because they shared with Gothic vaulting an elasticity which specially commended them in earthquake areas; hence Cali in Colombia constructed a *mudéjar* ceiling for its church as late as 1764. Renaissance and even Romanesque features continued till surprisingly late. Such conservatisms were common in Spain and Portugal themselves; naturally they were still more congenial in the colonies, where expatriates were peculiarly liable to want 'a church that looks like a church' (as the catch-phrase of modern conservatives in ecclesiastical architecture has it), that is, like the parish church of their childhood memories (Newcomb: pl. vii, 3; Kubler 1941: 209-299; Marianno Filho; Prat-Puig; Ángulo 1947; Harvey: 83, 104-107; Ángulo 1955: 83-141, 206-225, 540-543; 1950: 16-19; Kubler/Soria: 62-105; Bazin 1964, 1974: 224; Toussaint 1967: 79-127; Fernández 1969: 73, 83 and pls 53-120; Castedo: 104-106; Marco Dorta 1973: 15-285).

Then, there are some European national influences other than the Iberian. In Latin America, as in India, the extreme stretching of Iberian man-power meant that missionaries from other countries had to be admitted; in the Spanish colonies and still more in Brazil there were areas of marked German and Italian influence (Buschiazzo 1946/7; Bury 1955; Bazin 1956, 1958; Plattner; Palm 1966: 41, 43; Camacho; Sitwell; Gasparini 1967:11; Marco Dorta 1973: 299-328). There were even features imported from or influenced by China, notably the great choir-screen at México Cathedral, made at Macao of bronze alloyed with silver and gold (Buschiazzo 1946/7; McCall; Toussaint 1948, 1961; Bazin 1956: 127, 144; 1958: pls 40, 42; Cali: 30, 123, 125; Rojas 1963: pl. 69; Vasconcellos: 42, 45, 50; Castedo: 125, 156, 158, 161, 162, 188, 192; Marco Dorta 1973: 189-191; Cameron: 89). There was a regular traffic in cult-objects from China *via* the Manila galleons.

Another variant was the development in some places and times of the fortress-church. Churches built in whole or part for defence, or for incorporation into defences, were not unknown in Europe; but in the less settled colonial conditions they naturally had greater advantages, though their construction was discouraged by official disapproval from Spain (Zapatero: 19, 36). Notably in the early Mexican settlements before the Indians were fully cowed, and later near the Yucatán coasts exposed to piratical attacks, and in the wilder parts of Bolivia adjacent to unconquered tribes, churches tended to be solidly built, with battlements and narrow windows, and forming, with their attached convents and *plazas*, defensive units (Toussaint 1967: 78, 82, 99; Zawisza: 94, 120; Castedo: 104-106; Hayes: 29, 52, 59; Marco Dorta 1973: 26-50).

Another important development in America of something not unknown but very rare in Europe was the *'capilla abierta'* or 'open chapel', with its allied *'posas'*, which proliferated in Mexico for a few years between 1540 and 1555, and then ceased. The 'open chapel', often of great beauty, was a vaulted sanctuary over an altar, with the western arch opening not to a nave but to the town *plaza*; it seems to have been intended to house the Mass in the view of Indian converts, either temporally, till the great convent church could be built, or permanently, for the specially large throngs at major festivals; its builder may or may not have considered that such a place of worship helpfully recalled pre-Conquest open-air cults. The associated *posas* were small, generally altarless, open chapels at the corners of the *plaza*, intended as resting-places during processions. In Perú and Chile there was also for three centuries a liking for *posas* at the corners of the church *atrios*; but there and elsewhere, notably in New Mexico, the place of the ground-level open chapel was taken by a balcony over the main door in the church *façade*, entered from the upper *coro* (Kubler 1941: 305-422); Guerrero; Palm 1953; Ángulo 1955: 168-197, 214-218, 233-243; Mesa/Gisbert 1961; 1966: 15-23; Rojas 1963: 19-39 and pls 9-21; McAndrew; Toussaint 1967: 26-31, 42, 85-90, 105, 119, 125, 256; Fernández 1969: 66; Castedo: 105, 107; Zawisza; Marco Dorta 1973: 27-53, 81-82, 94, 236-238, 285-286; Gisbert: 140-169).

Yet another marked variation in the colonies from the metropolitan Baroque is in the very frequent flattening of the ornamental features. This, in America, used to be ascribed to influence from pre-Conquest forms; but actually it is an all-but-universal feature of provincial work by the semi-trained, occurring even in remoter parts of Spain and Portugal themselves. In the Iberian colonies it is very common right from Orotava in Tenerife, across America, to Goa in India; perhaps it was largely due to new craftsmen working from engravings rather than from stone-yard tradition.

There was also a general broadening and thickening of design, especially in those many parts of the colonies where this helped as a precaution against earthquakes. Such 'earthquake Baroque' (already noted in the Philippines) accentuated a coarsening which would anyhow have occurred in provincial work.

Along with all this, a wide range of locally variant schools developed as time went on, each based on its own city centre, just as local schools had arisen throughout Europe during many preceding centuries. Generally the variations were in comparative details; but in some areas local conditions led to the development of very distinctive regional styles. In parts of Mexico and in the southern States of the U.S.A., the use of adobe, with its logical consequence of plain, thick, tapering walls, made churches which look thoroughly at home in their *pueblos* (Kubler 1940, 1972; Bunting 1964, 1974, 1976; Marco Dorta 1973: 190-193; Hayes). In the South American forest area the availability of enormous trees, together with an absence of lime, led to churches (now almost all destroyed) of a most distinctive type, in which the roof was carried entirely by wooden pillars, the adobe walls being mere infilling for privacy (Kubler/Soria: 100; Buschiazzo; 1963: 173-190; Plá; Marco Dorta 1973: 308-317). Incidentally, the history of the Forest Missions provides an account of what must be the strangest use ever made of art on the mission field. In 1995 Fr José Cabarta, S.J., was travelling near the Río Meta, when he was confronted by the local *cacique*, a relapsed convert, resolved on his murder. But the Father was carrying under his arm a rolled-up picture of St Francis Xavier, and when the would-be assassin saw this he took it to be a new type of gun and fled forthwith (Goodman: 89-90).

In this account of many types of variation from the European norm in Latin American architecture, the remarkable thing is that nothing has been said about elements derived from the great pre-Conquest building art; this is because there is practically no such influence. Sometimes ancient foundations were used for the churches, notably at Cuzco (Marco Dorta 1973: 69, 72-73); and at Willka Waman, not far from that city, there is even a church largely made out of the fabric of an Inca temple (Gasparini 1974). Indian craftsmen frequently inserted local faces and flora and fauna into their decorations, and sometimes even Aztec and Inca mythical animals. The old craft of feather-mosaic was used for church vestments and pictures, often sent as presents to European prelates (Pls XL, 1, 2) (Toussaint 1967: 72-74; Anders, etc.; Cameron: 2, 4). Local exigencies led to other strange uses of indigenous materials, as when church pictures in the Spanish areas of the U.S.A. were painted on buffalo-hide instead of canvas (Hayes: 40-41). The famous image of Our Lady of Guadalupe (1527) portrays a woman in some respects Indian (actually she was replacing an Indian virgin goddess who had had her temple on that site), and is painted on a peasant's *tilma*; there is even one Mexican colonial-period Madonna who is shown as grinding maize. The greatest of all Colonial painters, Melchor Pérez de Holguín of Potosí (*c.* 1660 - *post* 1724), once painted the Madonna as a girl in Indian dress washing clothes on the local kind of scrubbing-board (Mesa/Gisbert 1956: 143-145 and pl. lxxv; Kubler/Soria: 325; Marco Dorta 1973: 376 and fig. 613). In these and similar ways there was a good deal of what can be called spontaneous indigenization (García Granados; Neumayer; Bazin 1964, 1974: 223-224; Mesa/Gisbert 1966: 33-102; Fernández 1969: 59, 68; Markman 1974).

Nevertheless, in all the official and ecclesiastical art of this period there is never anything that can be called a survival or intermingling of the pre-Conquest styles. This holds even of the peasant work in *santos* and *bultos* which approximates to folk-art (Pls XLI, 2, 3; XLII, 1, 2) (Anon. *Handlist*; *El Palacio*; Anon. *Plateria*; Anon. *Arte Religiosa*; Meireles; Valladeres; Santos, Marquês de; Dorner; Firpi; Ahlborn; Toussaint 1967: 382-397; 1974: 202-212). The old civilizations had simply been submerged. Church designs were always in clerical hands or at least under strict clerical supervision; and in the background was the Inquisition, alert for pagan survivals. The craftsmen were organized in guilds which in some places were jealously guarded European preserves; elsewhere *mestizos* and even Indians were admitted to the guilds, and some of them rose to eminence as architects and painters and sculptors; yet even so they worked along lines as strictly European as if they had been of pure white race.

Because of all this, most critics have now abandoned '*mestizo*' as an aesthetic term. Yet perhaps the reaction against it has gone too far. There was indeed no blend of Iberian and pre-Conquest cultures; but there was a blend of Iberian and Indian sensibilities. Despite all the initial imports—*e.g.*, good masters like Alonso Vázquez emigrated to Mexico; the great Zurbarán ran a prolific export trade from his studio to a relative in Perú; there was a constant import of engravings; even a whole church was taken stone by stone as ship's ballast from Portugal to Brazil—and despite all the sedulous copying in correct Mannerist or Baroque style, still the infiltration of indigenous features and the development of regional forms led in time to an art which, when at its liveliest, did not indeed copy anything pre-Conquest, but nevertheless expressed the indigenous mentality. In Mexico the profusion of polychromy adorning an already ornate carving ('ultra-Baroque'; Toussaint's 'exuberant Baroque') had nothing to do with Aztec forms, yet reflected the old Aztec feeling. The flatness, yet the overflowing vitality and richness of ornament, amounting to a *horror vacui*, and the other characteristics of Latin American Baroque, can all individually be explained in terms of pure Europeanism, *plus* the garishness associated with the *nouveaux riches* the world over; but they add up to a change in spirit which is based on a mixture of races in blood and psychology. This new spirit found its outlet not so much in painting, which remained mostly mediocre, or even in architecture, despite much magnificence, but mainly in sculpture. In Mexico some of the crucifixes and saints in ecstasy, and in Brazil the tremendous carvings of the diseased mulatto cripple Antônio Francisco Lisbôa, 'O Aleijadinho' (1738-1814), who in his last years could carve only with hammer and chisel strapped to his arms, exude an unequalled *terribilità*, a *tremendismo* (Freudenfeld; Marianno Filho 1945, 1961; Bury 1949, 1949; Jorge; Kelemen 1951, 1967: 248-255; Anon. *A. F. Lisboa*; Kubler/Soria: 194-196; Bazin 1956: 186-190; 1958: pls 85, 91; 1964, 1974: 223-224; Mann; Castedo: 194-199). Works of this kind, and not any alleged hybrids, show the truest *mestizismo* (Castedo: pt ii; *Boletín* 12; Burland: 221-222; Marco Dorta 1973: 24, 41-42, 170-192, 204, 270, 280-293, 323).

It is perhaps surprising that after the Colonial period until quite modern times, despite the fierce national political nationalisms unleashed, the arts of the new republics were little but cold copies of European models in neo-Classical, neo-Gothic and Eclectic. But recently Latin America as a whole has taken the world lead in developments of the 'international' ferro-concrete architecture, and Mexico in the arts of mosaic and fresco; and in these various media truly national styles have begun to appear, at any rate in secular work.

The mainly Northern Europeans who colonized Canada and the northern parts of the U.S.A. brought their own various European styles with them, producing therewith a hotchpotch of mainly derivative and undistinguished work. An exception was in the 17th- and 18th-century churches of New England and the south-eastern States of the U.S.A., which in brick, wood, plaster, shingles and white paint often achieved a lovely blend of simplicity, grace and dignity (Sinnott). Some of their distinctive features are due to local social circumstances and availability of materials, but they contain no elements whatever from the indigenous Indian cultures, not even when special meeting-houses were built for 'praying Indians' who observed some relics of the old cults (Sinnott: 205-206).

In recent times, however, there has been, partly through church patronage and partly spontaneously, some indigenizing of Christian art in the surviving tribes of North America, associated with the revival of communal spirit in them (Pl. XLIII, 1) (Lehmann 1955: pls 175-178; 1966, 1969: pls 73-82; Cerny). The Eskimos have a traditional craft of small carvings in stone and morse, and a few of these depict Christian personages and scenes: this work is now being professionally marketed—an excellent thing in some ways, but also fraught with the dangers of 'airport art' (Lehmann 1966, 1969: pls 68-72). Much new art by Canadian Amerinds harks back to their tribal legends (Cinadier); religious leaders of the Ojibway, some of them devout Christians, continue to produce birch-bark scrolls of pictographs which form the teaching notes of *shamans* preparing candidates for admission into the *Midéwewin* rites, with an intermingling of Christian and tribal symbols (Dewdney). The Anglican Diocese of the Arctic has built its new cathedral in *igloo* form (sitting rather incongruously, though, among cubic apartment-blocks) (Pl. XLI, 1), and has adorned many of its churches with pieces of Eskimo craftsmanship. Further West, the Cree Indians are reported as now desiring a wigwam style for their churches (but the unkind may point out that the English have anticipated them in this, at the Roman Catholic Metropolitan Cathedral of Liverpool!).

Popular arts in Mexico and elsewhere, particularly those of the dance and those which make festival-objects such as the sugar-skulls for All Souls' Day, have retained many elements from pre-Conquest cults (Ober: 291-297; Roys; Oakes; Dorner; Fernández 1970: pls 54-59; Tonemaya; Wachtel: 27-58, 152-165, 179-183, 228-233, 259-263, 266-268). (*Cf.* Pl. XLIV, 1).

In Haiti, Honduras, Colombia, Venezuela and Brazil there has been, during and after the Second World War, a veritable explosion of folk-art painting, by groups of all sorts of people, chiefly though not entirely working-class. History will have to sort out how much of this is a real upsurge of latent talent, and how much is just a cashing-in on a tourist market for colourfully naïve mementoes. As society in those parts is at least nominally Christian, many Christian themes occur in this output. Most of it is small-scale work on hardboard; but one set of artists was commissioned in 1950/1 to fresco completely the Episcopalian (Anglican) Cathedral of Port-au-Prince, Haiti. These frescoes, and many of the other paintings, are orthodoxly Christian, and are of sound quality (Lehmann 1966, 1969: pls 84-95; Rodman 1973: 101-105). But very many of the smaller, hardboard pictures are of *vaudou* themes, representing the strange myths that have arisen in a syncretism of Christianity with local Indian and perhaps also African cults (Pl. XLIII, 2). *Vaudou* seems to reach depths in the Caribbean personality which the foreign orthodoxy cannot touch; many give themselves to it wholly; few escape it altogether. It is said that the artist of the 'Last Judgment' in the cathedral, was, by the time he came to paint the devils in it, near enough to Christianity for him to say that the *Loas*, though they existed, were not important; then he suddenly saw the devils of his picture as the *Loas* chasing him for his blasphemy, and he went out of his mind. In a psychological situation like that, it is not surprising that the *vaudou* paintings often show a vital energy which makes the orthodox ones look staid and heavy in comparison (Rodman 1973: 61-105; Luzbetak: 239-41; Bachmann; Anon. *S. Amer. Country Art*). Surely there is a moral for Christianity in that—if only one could formulate exactly what it is!

In Perú, sundry traditional arts of pottery, weaving, painting and modelling have been handed down to a flourishing present: indeed, their commercial success is now actually endangering them. Some are still purely pagan, and as the handsome glazed bulls of Pukará, which hold the liquor at fertility-festivals; some are purely Christian (Pls XLIV 2; XLV); some mix Christianity with paganism (Pl. XLVI), and some, most charmingly, with secular life (Pls XLVII; XLVIII) (Petterson; *Kamaq*).

X. *Conclusion*

This study has sought to show how Christian art, in part of its expansion beyond Europe, has taken on many diverse forms, with varying degrees of accommodation to a wide gamut of cultures. There have been failures theologically, through misunderstandings or improper syncretisms; and failures artistically, in unlovely hybrids. Much—as indeed in Europe—has just been sound run-of-the-mill work. Occasionally the challenge of the encounters has kindled work of spiritual and artistic genius. The record has not been a bad one, in construction.

But was not this achieved, critics urge, at a high cost in destruction? One has indeed to admit that the invasions by Western culture, of which the Christian missions were one aspect, have wrought sad havoc in many indigenous civilizations. Some of this has been by sheer arrogant vandalism; even more has been by the less deliberate but wider effects of a sapping of the old securities and vitalities.

This reproach is often exaggerated. The Church has often softened the blows from other Western impacts; it has often helped to conserve the best in other cultures. In any case, no culture is ever static: look how the West is now busy at kicking away its own traditions! And, if new things are started, they cannot mature quickly: twelve centuries stretch between Galilee and Chartres: our survey here has barely covered five. There can still be hope that Christianity will bring life 'more abundantly', like 'a well of water springing up into everlasting life'.

The present is indeed confused. No one knows quite what to make, in religious art, of the impact of the new international techniques, or how to control or express new social modes and aspirations, or even how to manifest the renewal of old gospel simplicities; still less has the Church learned how to cope with the modern maelstrom of the general denial of any objective aesthetic standards. We stand in a welter of rival art-experiences, which is one aspect of the general loss of that solid social background out of which alone great art can arise. Yet there have been some modern gains. At least no one now can export Westernism with an unquestioned confidence that he is conferring the benefits of an indisputably higher civilization; on the other hand, the more naïve kinds of indigenization are now outdated, for, as Professor Bruno Bürki well puts it, '*nous ne voulons évidemment pas faire de nos églises des musées pour un folklore qui dans la vie ordinaire aurait perdu toute vitalité'*. The refutation of old errors does not indeed mean that they are no longer committed; still less does it mean that we already know the positive answers. But throughout the world nowadays there is a fine bubbling in the kneading-trough of Christian art; maybe the gospel leaven will yet produce a sweet loaf.

EXPLANATIONS OF THE PLATES

(References are according to the bibliographies of the relevant sections.)

Plate I, 1

A Fresco of 'Madonna and Child', from a Christian House in Aleppo. The fascinating set of Syrian Christian paintings from that house, now in the Islamisches Museum, Berlin, D.D.R., was signed by ʿĪsā ibn Buṭrus in Sept.-Oct. 1603: for details see Twair.
Courtesy of the Staatliche Museen zu Berlin, D.D.R.

Plate I, 2

'The Nativity' according to the Qu'rān. From a MS of *Qiṣaṣ al-Ambīyā* (*Stories of the Prophets*), late 16th cent., in the Chester Beatty Collection, Dublin (MS 231, f. 277). (A similar picture, early-17th-cent., is in Paris at the Bibliothèque Nationale (supp. persan 1313, f. 174).) In the Nativity story as related in the *Qu'rān* (xix: 22-27) Mary gave birth in a desert place, and in her exhaustion leaned against a withered palm-tree; this at her touch sprang into new leaf and showered down dates for her refreshment, and at its roots appeared a miraculous spring (here coloured black, through the tarnishing of the artist's original silver).
Courtesy of the Chester Beatty Collection.

Plate II, 1

A Page from a Book of Old Testament Illustrations, presented to Shāh ʿAbbās I. Pierpont Morgan Library, New York, M. 638, f. 24b, picturing the episodes of I Sam. 14: 37-45 and 15: 2-9. When Pope Clement VIII despatched an embassy to Shāh ʿAbbās I in 1604, he provided it with no presents for the Shāh, perhaps being disgusted with thefts from previous embassies. His envoys, knowing how futile, indeed insulting, an empty-handed embassy would be, themselves gathered a set of presents from sundry notables; among these was a magnificent 13th-cent. Parisian book of Old Testament illustrations, donated by the Cardinal-Bishop of Cracow, Bernard Maciejowski, on whom the embassy called when essaying the northern route to Persia *via* Russia. After many adventures the envoys finally reached Iṣfahān in December 1607; there the Shāh received them on 3rd January 1608, and, though making a few jokes about the depiction of the Devil, he was much impressed by the book, and against the Latin captions for each picture he had Persian captions put, not translations of the Latin, but new titles provided by the Fathers who composed the embassy. At some later time Hebrew transliterations (not translations) were added. The MS continued to have an adventurous history. See Cockerell, etc.
Courtesy of the Pierpont Morgan Library.

Plate II, 2

'The Descent of the Holy Spirit on Christ, Mary and Joseph', by Muḥammad (Paolo) Zamān. 14.5 × 21.2 cm. Signed in Arabic and dated as painted during 14 months in

1682/3. Leningrad, Institute for Oriental Studies, U.S.S.R. Album E. 14, 84. In the reign of Shāh ʿAbbās II (1642/66) an embassy was sent to Rome, which included the painter Muḥammad Zamān (c. 1630 - c. 1700), who was there converted. Returning to Persia as Paolo Zamān, he found it prudent to move to India, where the gossipy Manucci saw him when visiting Aurangzeb's Court from Kashmīr; he was then living as a Muslim but claimed still to hold the Christian faith; later he seems to have returned to Persia and there died as a Muslim. However, many modern authorities doubt Manucci's story. (See Arnold 1928, 1965: 148-9; Gray: 70; Ivanov 1962, etc.: Introd. and pls 83-5; Maclagan: 192, 235-6, 244; Martin: pl. 173; Martinovitch; Manucci; II, 17-8; Smith 1911: 466 and pl. cxvi; 1930: 217; 1962: 191.)

Courtesy of the Leningrad Branch of the Institute for Oriental Studies, U.S.S.R.

Plate III, 1

The Bethlehem Church, New Julfa. 1628/48. Interior, looking east. One of the finest of the Armenian churches in a suburb of Iṣfahān. A fully Western plan, with completely Persian architectural style and paintings imported from the West or locally executed in mixed style. For details, see Carswell 1968.

Courtesy of Professor John Carswell and the Oxford University Press (*New Julfa*).

Plate III, 2

The Bethlehem Church, New Julfa. 1628/48. Dome interior, looking north-west: a purely Persian masterpiece.

Courtesy of Professor John Carswell and the Oxford University Press (*New Julfa*).

Plate IV, 1

The Church of St Simon the Zealot, Shīrāz. 1937/8. Architect, Rev. Norman Sharp. The ten-centred Persian arch is used throughout. Most of the windows are of foreign glass made up in Persia, at Yazd, over a century ago. The chancel rails use a pattern from the front of the Great Mosque at Samarqand; the lectern, *prie-Dieu*, altar, reredos and other furnishings use similar ancient patterns. For full particulars, see Sharp.

Photo: Bp W. J. Thompson. Courtesy of the Church Missionary Society.

Plate IV, 2

'The Raising of the Widow of Cain's Son'. By Hajj Musavvir ul Mulk of Iṣfahān, the artist who revived the ancient Persian art of miniature painting. Born 1890, and at least in late 1975 still alive, though unable now to draw owing to paralysis of the right arm; a Muslim, but willing to accept Christian commissions. The face at the bottom right-hand corner is formed from the artist's signature. The lines below are couplets 4261 and 4262 from Book III of the *Mathnawī* of Jalāl al-Dīn Rūmī, the great Persian mystical poet, in praise of the episode from Luke 7:11-16 which is the subject of the drawing. The border is a design copied from a mosaic of glazed tiles in the great Karatāy College at Konya (Iconium), which was built in 1251, while Jalāl al-Dīn was a student there.

Courtesy of Rev. R. Norman Sharp, Mr Robin E. Waterfield and Messrs George Allen & Unwin.

Plate V, 1

The Façade of the Basilica of Bom Jesus, Velha Goa. The Jesuit church of 1594/1605, which has housed the body of St Francis Xavier since before his canonization in 1624.
  Photo: Author.

Plate V, 2

The Side of the Church of Nossa Senhora do Monte, Velha Goa. 16th-cent., refashioned in the (?) 18th cent. A church of gracious classical architecture. When the author saw it in 1949, the front porch was half walled off as a cowshed; he has heard recently that the church has been well restored architecturally, but also that it has been stripped of its fine interior furnishings by thieves for the antiques market.
  Photo: Author.

Plate VI, 1

The Sanctuary of the Church of N. S. da Expectação, Great St Thomas' Mount, Madras. The centre-piece is the famous 'Mylapore Cross', an (?) 8th-cent. carving, with a Pahlavi inscription, by 'Syrian' Christians of South India: it is paralleled only by half-a-dozen others in Kērala. Local tradition affirms that the Apostle Thomas was martyred over the cross on this very site, and that the red mark on it is the stain of his blood; in the 16th and 17th cents it was reported constantly to have sweated during Mass. In front of it is a Byzantine icon of the Virgin and Child, which has been there since 1558, even though it is not, as tradition says, by St Luke! Above it is an Indian Christian oil-painting of St Thomas' martyrdom, dating from before 1695. The gilt-and-white reredos, in typical Portuguese style, has an inscription in Armenian, recording its donation by a merchant of that nation who was a great benefactor of the local Catholics in the first half of the 18th cent. The double-headed eagle on the altar front refers to the Augustinian see of Mylapore. The over-arching Gothic vault is of the Portuguese church erected in 1547 on the site of earlier one of about 1521, which was itself built on the site of earlier Christian ruins. At the side are two modern statues of European *kitsch*.
  Courtesy of Rev. Fr V. M. Gnanapragasam, S.J., Tamil Research and Culture Centre, Loyola College, Madras.

Plate VI, 2

The Church of Nossa Senhora da Piedade, Divar, Ilhas, Goa. Second half of 18th cent. Rococo elegance.
  Courtesy of the American Institute of Indian Studies, Ramnagar, Varanasi.

Plate VII, 1

The Chapel of Our Lady, Mormugão Fort, Goa. C. 1550. A mere niche in a ramp leading up to the battlements; the congregation would have to stand in the open between it and a large stone cross at the outer edge of the fortified area. A typical piece of Romanesque-like archaizing in simple colonial work. This photograph was taken in 1949: it is now reported that the fort has disappeared in the modern development of Mormugão harbour.
  Photo: Author.

Plate VII, 2

The Santadurga Temple,Queulá, Pondá Dt,Goá. 18th cent. Laterite and plaster. European influence is very obvious in this and several other Hindu temples in what was once the Goa *enclave*. One also suspects Chinese influence in the eaves, and in the pagoda-like towers; these latter, however, may owe their peculiar form rather to their function as *dvipastambhas*, towers for the display of lights, such as are common in the adjacent Marāthī and Konkānī areas.

Courtesy of the American Institute of Indian Studies, Ramnagar, Varanasi.

Plate VIII, 1

The Church of the Holy Rosary, Tejgaon, Dacca, Bangladesh. The *façade* is a unique blend of Baroque and Bengālī. The church was built in 1677; a restoration in 1940 did no harm to the *façade,* but unhappily it took away the mouldings of alternating arcs and triangles over the aisle windows, which had given character to the side elevation (Costantini 270).

Courtesy of Fr Richard Timm, C.S.C., Dacca.

Plate VIII, 2

A Credence Table from the Jesuit Church, Lahore. Victoria and Albert Museum, London (I.S. 15-1882). 107 × 82½ cm. 1610/20. Typical Indo-Portuguese inlay work (ebony, stained ivory, bone and lac, in rosewood). A quaint mixture of Christian and Indian motifs.

Reproduced by permission of the Victoria and Albert Museum.

Plate IX

An Indian Textile 'Crucifixion'. Victoria and Albert Museum, London (I.S. 3-1953). 137 × 102 cm. Painted cotton from the Coromandel Coast, probably Pondicherry. Second half of 18th cent.

Reproduced by permission of the Victoria and Albert Museum.

Plate X, 1

'Virgin and Child': A Goanese Ivory. C. 1700. About 23 cm. high. Hair, robe edges and pattern, *etc.,* coloured and gilt. The statuette is in general of a very common Baroque type, but with Indianization of features and dress (though the *sārī* in some of its forms is in any case very like the traditional Western Madonna's robe). Before Oct. 1969 at Stonyhurst College, Lancashire; now in U.S.A.

Photo: Pye, Clitheroe. Courtesy of the Rector, Stonyhurst College.

Plate X, 2

'The Good Shepherd': A Goanese Ivory. Victoria and Albert Museum, London (A. 58-1949). 43 cm. high. 16th-cent. (?). The elaborate crowd of figures represent (reading downwards): (1) The Holy Ghost as a Dove; (2) God the Father; (3) Christ as the Good Shepherd, but asleep by a tree (showing assimilation to the Kṛṣṇa stories); (4) the Virgin and St John, flanking the Fountain of Life, with sheep; (5) Mary Magdalene, in a common Western pose, but here recalling the Hindu 'Sleeping Vishṇu'; (6) sundry animals; (7) the Apostles represented as sheep (as in early Western mosaics). This strange kind of ivory

is quite common: the author has come across examples of it at the Vatican, Lisbon, Funchal (Madeira), London, Cardiff and even at Burnley (Lancashire).

Reproduced by permission of the Victoria and Albert Museum.

Plate XI, 1

'*Fr Rudolf Aquaviva and Another Jesuit Debating with Muslim Divines before Akbar*': *A Mughal Miniature*. Chester Beatty Collection, Dublin (MS 3, f. 263v). C. 1605. Painted by Narsingh for Akbar's own copy of the *Akbarnāma*. Aquaviva is identified by the inscription 'Pādrī Rodolf, one of the Nazarene sages'; the other must be Antonio Monserrate or Francisco Henriques. The scene is Akbar's '*Ibādat-khāna*, where such debates were frequent.

Courtesy of the Chester Beatty Collection.

Plate XI, 2

'*Christ's Entry into Jerusalem*': *A Mughal Miniature*. British Museum, London (1965-7-24-05). 15 × 7½ cm. This is one of the illustrations to a very early copy of Jerome Xavier's illustrated Persian *Life of Christ*, which was presented to Akbar in 1602. Indian background architecture; Portuguese dress. The portrayal of two asses, both saddled, and of different sizes, is due to an overliteral understanding of the repetition involved in the Hebrew poetic form of Zech. 9:9, as quoted in Matt. 21:5!

Reproduced by permission of the Trustees of the British Museum.

Plate XII

'*Nūr Jahān in a Palace Pavilion*', entertaining Jahāngīr and Shāh Jahān or some other prince in 1617. Victoria and Albert Museum, London (I.M. 115-1921). 39 × 28 cm. The picture used to be dated *c.* 1670, but is now held to be an early-19th-cent. copy of an early-17th-cent. original. The style of painting, the theme, and the architecture represented, are all pure Indian; but there can be seen, on a minute scale but with great clarity in the original, the pictures on the pavilion wall, and these are mainly European; they include some portraits, but also a 'Madonna' and an '*Ecce Homo*'.

Reproduced by permission of the Victoria and Albert Museum.

Plate XIII

'*The Martyrdom of St Cecilia*': *A Mughal Painting*. Victoria and Albert Museum, London (I.M. 139-1921). 15 × 11½ cm. By Nīnī. C. 1610. The charming colouring of the painting is by the Indian artist; otherwise it is a close copy of the Wierix (Pl. XIV, 1), apart from some Indianization of features and details. The picture is let into a specimen of the writing of Sultān 'Alī Mashadī, a well-known calligraphist of the 15th cent.

Reproduced by permission of the Victoria and Albert Museum.

Plate XIV, 1

'*The Martyrdom of St Cecilia*': *An Engraving by Jerome Wierix*. British Museum, London (Album III of Collection of Wierix Prints: 1859-7-9-3192). 13 × 10¼ cm. Hieronymus Wierix of Antwerp (*c.* 1553 - *c.* 1619) and his brother Johan (1549 - *post* 1615) were among the principal sources of the religious engravings so much in demand by contemporary missionaries throughout the world. The original is unknown; but the figure of St Cecilia is based on the famous statue by Stefano Maderna, which lies over her body in her church at Trastévere, Rome. The church is on the site of her house where she was martyred; the statue is said to have been modelled from the actual body, as seen by the sculptor when the original tomb in the catacombs was opened in 1599.

Reproduced by permission of the Trustees of the British Museum.

Plate XIV, 2

'*The Virgin and Child*': *An Engraving by Gilles Sadeler, after Mazzola-Bedoli.* British Museum, London (51-3-8-1027). 12.3 × 10 cm. A fairly close copy of the original oil, by Girolamo Mazzola-Bedoli, a relative, pupil and collaborator of the much-better-known master Parmigianino (München, Alte Pinakothek, 5289), though with St Bruno omitted, the wall altered, and the floral foreground fussily added to. In this, and in several other versions possessed by the British Museum, the picture is attributed to Parmigianino. Gilles (Egidius, *etc.*) Sadeler (1575-1629) and his brothers Jan and Raphael were engravers whose work was frequently copied in India.

Reproduced by permission of the Trustees of the British Museum.

Plate XIV, 3

'*The Virgin and Child*': *A Mughal Painting after Sadeler's Engraving* from the oil by Mazzola-Bedoli. India Office Library, London (Johnson Coll., XIV.2). 14 × 10½ cm. Much coarser drawing than in another, very delicate, copy in the Bodleian Library, Oxford (MS Douce or. b. 1. f. 1), and with heavy colouring which is in no way related to that of the original oil.

Reproduced by permission of the Librarian, India Office Library and Records.

Plate XV, 1

'*The Last Supper (?)*': *A Mughal Painting.* India Office Library, London (Johnson Coll., VI. st. 6). 17 × 10 cm. Portuguese dresses. The subject is so imaginatively handled that some take the picture to be of 'The Marriage at Cana'. Another (very similar) version from the same (unknown) prototype was sold at Sotheby's on 27th Nov. 1974, from the Warren Hastings Album in the Phillipps Collection; in the catalogue of that sale (pl. 39) it was called a 'Marriage at Cana' and dated mid-17th-cent.

Reproduced by permission of the Librarian, India Office Library and Records.

Plate XV, 2

'*Adoration of the Virgin and Child (?)*': *A Mughal Painting.* Bodleian Library, Oxford (MS Douce or.c.4.24). Pre-1834. 25¼ × 17 cm. Very fanciful: it appears to be a Mass with the Host and Chalice replaced by the Virgin and Child, and the foreground figures defy interpretation.

Reproduced by permission of the Bodleian Library, Oxford.

Plate XVI, 1

'*S. Paolo fuori le Mura*': *A Piranesi Engraving*. From *Vedute di Roma*, 1748, *etc*. The basilica is of course shown as it was before it was destroyed by fire in 1823 and subsequently rebuilt.

Reproduced by permission of the British Library Board.

Plate XVI, 2

'*S. Paolo fuori le Mura*': *An Indian Painting after Piranesi*. Privately owned in U.S.A. A drawing with touches of bright colour. By a Goanese or Gujarātī artist, who has reversed the picture, has put some of the figures, both on the floor and in the wall-pictures, in the dress of Western Indian hill-tribes, and has turned the cross on the high altar into a small *liṅgam*! He has also badly misunderstood the more foreshortened of the triforia, the shadows of the pillars on the floor, and the brackets of the roof-rafters.

Courtesy of Messrs Hartnoll & Eyre, London.

Plate XVII, 1

'*The Virgin and Child, with a European Drinking Party*': *A Mughal Painting*. Islamisches Museum, Berlin, D.D.R. (I.4595.f.10). 17th-cent. The crazy appearance of the chair is due to Islamic perspective having been applied to the very difficult subject of a chair set at an angle. The figure with the book cannot be identified. Even if (what is disputed) the two parts of the picture are meant to be read together, probably no disrespect to the Christian religion is intended: the artist had simply made a statement of contemporary Portuguese interests in India as they appeared to him.

Courtesy of the Staatliche Museen zu Berlin, D.D.R.

Plate XVII, 2

The Temple of Vishṇu, Kālīghāt, Calcutta. A curious blend of East and West.

Photo: the late F. Deaville Walker. Courtesy of the Methodist Church, Overseas Division, London.

Plate XVIII, 1

A Temple Maṇḍapam. On the roof of a hall in one of the major temples at Kāñci (Conjeeveram). Its purpose was to be a resting-place for the image of the deity during processions (hence the central stone platform). The use of European classical architectural forms is typical of the late period.

Photo: Author.

Plate XVIII, 2

The Jebalayam (Prayer-Room, Chapel), Kristu-kula Āśrama, Tirupattur, S. India. 1928/32. The use of the large and non-functional *vimana* over the shrine, as in the local temples, is an expensive device, but was essential to the purpose of the founders of the *āśrama*, Drs S. Jesudason and Forrester-Paton, to express its identification with the life of its neighbourhood; there has, however, been a careful avoidance of the imagery which often runs riot over such buildings, so as to make no suggestion of idolatry.

Photo: Dr Frank Lake. Courtesy of the Church Missionary Society, London.

Plate XIX, 1

The West Front of Dornakal Cathedral, Church of South India (ex-Anglican). Built in 1939 by Bishop V. Azariah, the first Anglican bishop of Indian race, to his own design (with assistance from Canon, later Bishop, T. H. Cashmore). Bishop Azariah chose a mixed Hindu/Muslim style in order to express his Church's identification with all aspects of Indian culture: he also deliberately gave the building some magnificence, in order to provide a counterweight to the desperate individual poverty and consequent inferiority complex of the Christian converts of his diocese, who were mostly outcastes.

Photo: Rev. H. G. Korteling, Punganur, Chittoor Dt. Courtesy of the Methodist Church, Overseas Division, London.

Plate XIX, 2

A Temple Maṇḍapam at Kañci. This type of open building is common within and around the enclosures of the temples at the great pilgrimage-centres in South India. It is thus thoroughly within the tradition of religious building around Madras; but those who adapt it for Christian prayer-rooms in India may not always recall that within Hinduism *maṇḍapams* are not the normal places for worship; rather they are used for pilgrim shelters, ceremonial meals and dances, lectures on the *Vedas*, and similar peripheral purposes.

Photo: Author.

Plate XX, 1, 2

A Maquette by the late Fr H. Heras, S.J., for a scheme of adaptation to Christian purposes of a medium-sized South Indian temple (though the towers are of the Orissan rather than the Southern type). This maquette was displayed at the great Vatican Exhibition of Missionary Art in 1949, and in other ways was publicized by the late Cardinal Celso Costantini; but some ten years later it was seen by the author gathering dust in a locked attic at the Lateran Museum. The Spanish Jesuit Fr Heras was one of the most notable Indian church historians of his day.

Courtesy of Fides.

Plate XXI, 1

'The Temptation of Christ', by Alfred D. Thomas. Born in Āgra, educated at the Lucknow School of Art, under Abanindranāth Tagore, and in London and Italy, A. D. Thomas is perhaps the best-known of the modern Indian Christian painters, partly because of the early publicizing of his work by the S.P.G. (now U.S.P.G.) and his long residence in London. His work, however, has a sensuous softness which some feel owes more to a type of Buddhism than to Christianity. Notably in the present scene, Jesus is shown with an impassivity more akin to that of Buddha than to the spirit of the Gospels; and the introduction of a sexual element into one of the Temptations of Christ makes that akin to one which is related as following the Great Enlightenment of the Buddha, but this element is not found at all in the Gospels (though Tintoretto's 'Temptation' in the Scuola di San Rocco at Venice comes near to it).

Courtesy of the U.S.P.G., London.

Plate XXI, 2

'*Tamil Christmas*', *by Sr Geneviève*, of St Mary's Convent, Bangalore. Christmas card published by Art India, Pune. Modernized folk-art style.
Courtesy of Art India.

Plate XXII, 1

'*This is Christ the King*', *by Angelo da Fonseca*, perhaps the best-known of the modern Roman Catholic Indian artists. Born Goa, 1902; died 1968. Christmas card published by Art India, Pune. Neo-Mughal.
Courtesy of Art India.

Plate XXII, 2

'*It is the Lord!*', *by Jyoti Sahi*. Born in 1944 by an English mother to an Indian father, and now living with an English wife near Bangalore, South India, Jyoti Sahi was trained in art by a pupil of Abanindranāth Tagore and also at London; he then learned Indian philosophy at a Hindu *āśrama* in Kērala. After having experimented in sundry styles, he now concentrates on paintings that use esoteric symbols, mainly those traditional in Hindu sacramental art. This picture is based on the account in John 21:1-14 of the post-Resurrection miraculous draught of fishes; it uses the Hindu symbols of the triangle and the circle (the fishes and the net thus arranged), and refers especially to the cry of Peter in verse 7, and to the mystic number of 153 fishes in verse 11 (153 = 1 + 2 ..... 17; 17 = 10 + 7—the number thus symbolizing perfection).
Courtesy of Art India and Missio.

Plate XXIII, 1

'*Tujhe Praṇām*', *by Jamini Roy*. The title is Hindi for 'Hail', referring to Luke 1:28. Christmas card published by Art India, Pune. Jamini Roy was born in 1887 in West Bengāl, and died in 1972. He was one of the most famous of modern Indian painters; he absorbed influences from Tagore, Kālīghāt painting, Santal tribal life, and, although he was never a Christian, Christ. The 'fish-eyes' so prominent in the picture have been interpreted as a use of Hindu symbolism for the intensity of a devotee's contemplation of God, or of God's constant watchfulness; but Taylor: 64-5 reports that the artist himself had told him that 'he had never heard of these ideas'; and indeed parallels from Africa and Central and Southern America would suggest that they are merely a widespread convention of 'primitive' art.
Courtesy of Art India.

Plate XXIII, 2

Christmas thoroughly Indianized, and also thoroughly Secularized! A commercial Christmas card, 1957.
Courtesy of Sri S. K. Isaac.

Plate XXIV

'*The Crucifixion*', *from the Film 'The Cross and the Lotus*', which was produced in 1973 by Gateway Film Productions Limited (London and Bristol) for the Church of South

India and a group of associated British Churches. Note the *pottu* on the dancer's forehead in the form of a cross; this is an ingenious attempt to Christianize a female adornment which has been the cause of much heart-searching in the South Indian Church: as in South India the *pottu* is put on by all women except those of ill repute, a Christian girl does not want to leave it off; but as it is made partly of temple ash (though it is *not*, as is commonly supposed in the West, a caste-mark), it is theologically suspect.

Courtesy of Gateway Film Productions Limited and the Overseas Council of the Church of Scotland.

Plate XXV, 1

'Dives and Lazarus (?)', in a Javanese Version. John Rylands University Library of Manchester (MS Jav. 6, derived from the Bibliotheca Lindesiana). *C.* 1750. 30.5 × 20.4 cm. One of the $11\frac{1}{2}$ delicately coloured drawings which fill some of the 25 frames in the text of a paper MS of a *Lives of the Prophets.* Though this is a book of Muslim traditions, yet some of the illustrations are clearly influenced by a set of Bible pictures. Thus, this picture, and the one following it in the MS, though illustrating an episode in the life of Idrīs, a prophet who lived before Noah, seems based on some Christian prints of the gospel parable in Luke 16:19-31 (a parable which, coincidentally, seems to have complex oriental origins).

Courtesy of the John Rylands University Library of Manchester.

Plate XXV, 2

Phat-Diem Cathedral. Built by Don Luc Tran ('Père Six': 1825/99) as his parish church in 1875/95. 85 × $24\frac{1}{2}$ × $18\frac{1}{4}$ m. The site was a marsh, the foundations being beams driven 30 m. deep. The ironwood roof rests on 48 ironwood pillars. The side-walls are panels which can be moved away for overflow congregations on feast-days. (For details, see Olichon; Costantini: 254-60.)

Courtesy of Fides.

Plate XXVI, 1

A Burmese Crib. Victoria and Albert Museum, London (I.M. 16-1915). $30\frac{1}{2}$ × 19 × 39 cm. The Infant Christ is an Indo-Portuguese ivory of the 18th cent.; He wears a jewelled crown, belt and sandals of Burmese make, 18th or early-19th cent.; He lies in an ornate Portuguese gilt bedstead, in the style of Dom Pedro II (1683/1706), with bedding of 18th-cent. Brussels bobbin lace hung with pendant jewels; the tester is hung with tiny models of the Instruments of the Passion and household articles, curiously intermingled; the whole was put together around 1800.

Reproduced by permission of the Victoria and Albert Museum.

Plate XXVI, 2

A Kayon or Gunungan, of traditional form, as used to divide the scenes in Javanese shadow-plays. This has on one side (shown here) a Christ Crucified adored by angels, on a jungle background; on the other side is a Satan's head (in place of the customary fire-symbol or Element). It was made for use in the *Wayang Wahjn (Sacred Wayang)*, a play designed by Mgr Albert Sugijapranata, S.J., Archbishop of Semarang.

Courtesy of the Indonesisch Ethnografisch Museum, Delft.

Plate XXVII, 1

A Chinese Chasuble. Victoria and Albert Museum, London (1962-1899). Early-17th-cent. White silk, the ground filled with Chinese birds and flowers, embroidered in coloured silks and gold thread, with European-style stitches. On the orphrey, front and back, a 'Virgin and Child' copied from a European print. Worked by a Chinese craftsman.

Reproduced by permission of the Victoria and Albert Museum.

Plate XXVII, 2

'Ricci and the Chinese Convert "Ly Paulus" ': An Etching by Wencislaus Hollar. Author's Collection. 29 × 21 cm. Both Ricci and Ly Paulus are dressed as mandarins; yet note the European-style crucifix on, and 'Madonna' over, the altar. 'Ly Paulus Great Colaus' is Li Ying-shih, a mandarin astrologer who was one of Ricci's earliest converts, being baptized as Paul in 1602. Wenzel (Wencislaus) Hollar (1607/77) was a native of Prague, who worked as an artist mainly in England, in the service of the Earl of Arundel and other Catholic noblemen; he is best known for his almost contemporary etching of Shakespeare's Globe Theatre. The present etching of Ricci and Paulus is best known through the use of an engraving apparently made from it, with minor variations, as one of the pictures in Athanasius Kircher, S.J.'s famous book *China Illustrata* (Amsterdam, 1667). A very similar print is published by M. Beurdeley; fig. 93, from his collection in Paris, with the statement that it is after a painting in the Observatory of Zikanwei.

Photo: Roger David, Swansea, Wales.

Plate XXVIII

A Chinese Version of 'Nuestra Señora de l'Antigua'. In 1597 the Jesuit art school in Japan published a copper-plate print after a Jerome Wierix engraving of the famous 14th-cent. cult-image fresco in Seville Cathedral. In 1606 Ch'eng Ta Yueh, a well-known Chinese *littérateur*, published a woodcut copy of this Japanese print, along with three other Christian pictures, in his book *Ch'eng shih mo-yüan* (*Mr Ch'eng's Ink Remains*); the four pictures had been presented to him by Ricci at official request. 'Chu ti'en' above the picture means 'Lord of Heaven', a synonym for 'Christ' in this book.

Courtesy of the Percival David Foundation, University of London.

Plate XXIX, 1

'The Baptism of Christ': A Chinese Plate. Musée Guimet, Paris. Early-17th-cent. (Ch'ing dynasty). The Chinese porcelain-painter has copied a European print faithfully, even to an attempt at reproducing the script of the text-reference Matt. 3:16; but he seems to have been psychologically unable to depict poverty as other than brutish: this is clearer in some other versions—there being similar plates at the British Museum, London (Franks Coll. 597), Edinburgh, Amsterdam and doubtless elsewhere.

Courtesy of the Musée Guimet.

Plate XXIX, 2

'The Crucifixion': A Chinese Plate and Cup. British Museum, London (Franks Coll.). 1720/30. Grisaille, with gilt touches. After an engraving by Merian. Slight Sinicizing of faces and clouds. The design is another common one; there are other examples in Edinburgh, Amsterdam, the Author's Collection, and doubtless elsewhere. A companion piece shows the Resurrection. In this case the Chinese artist has not given an impression of degradation, but neither has he shown any nobility—only complete expressionlessness. The subject depicted raises a problem about these Christian pieces, in an acute form: For what purpose, of what purchasers, were such pieces intended? The use of plates as wall-plaques is modern; of cups, unknown. To eat or drink from such ware seems perverse. Despite modern scepticism about it, there is much to be said for the suggestion of Père d'Entrecolles, S.J., who had himself been stationed at the porcelain works, and who, writing from Peking in 1712, said that up to about 1695 they had been made so as to be slipped into consignments of porcelain to Japan and thus smuggle some Christian art to the Church in its bitter persecution there.

Reproduced by permission of the Trustees of the British Museum.

Plate XXX

'*Adam and Eve*': *A Chinese Cup*. Author's Collection. 18th-cent. Drawing in black and reddish, with colour-touches in gilt, reddish-brown and greenish-brown. Obviously from a European print, but copied by a Chinese painter with little experience of the nude and a crude idea of it.

Photo: Roger David, Swansea, Wales.

Plate XXXI, 1

Luke Ch'en: '*The Flight into Egypt*'. A typical picture by Card. Celso Costantini's chief protégé. Born 1903, as Ch'en Yüan Tu, in S. China, he came to Peking in 1920, and was soon established as a leading painter, working till 1923 in the home of his teacher. In 1928 he began to receive commissions for paintings of Christian subjects from the Apostolic Delegate; in 1932, while still professor of art at the Hua-Pei College, he was made head of Costantini's new Art Academy at the Catholic University, Peking. He was baptized at Easter 1932, as Lukas Ch'en, and was reported as still living in 1950.

Courtesy of Missio.

Plate XXXI, 2

Lin Ho Pei: '*The Storm on the Sea of Galilee*'. Matt. 6:23-7 and parallels.
Courtesy of Missio.

Plate XXXII, 1

'*The Parable of the Importunate Widow*'. Luke 18:1-8. One of a set of illustrations of the Parables, brought to England in 1948, made by a Chinese artist who had then recently been a patient at the C.M.S. Hospital at Putien, Fukien. The series gives the Parables a completely Chinese setting, though with Western technique; and it admirably brings out the important though often neglected fact that many of the gospel Parables are funny stories.

Courtesy of the Church Missionary Society, London.

Plate XXXII, 2

A Modern Roman Catholic Church in Taiwan. Modern Western materials and technique, but with lines harmonizing with those of the local buildings.
Courtesy of Fides.

Plate XXXIII, 1

Lukas Hasegawa, 'Mary as Patroness of the Japanese Martyrs'. Collection of the Päpstliches Werk der Glaubensverbreitung, Aachen. Part of a silk-painting by a modern Japanese artist (1897-1967), of what is a favourite theme in the Japanese Church.
Courtesy of the Päpstliches Werk der Glaubensverbreitung, Aachen.

Plate XXXIII, 2

A Buddhist Figure, with Christian Symbols at the Back. From the Japanese persecution-period.
Courtesy of Dom François de Grunne, O.S.B., and *Art d'Eglise*, Monastère Saint-André, Ottignies, Belgium.

Plate XXXIV, 1

A Cross with a Buddha-figure. Collection of Prof. Arno Lehmann, Halle. Persecution-period Japanese work. The cross copies a common European pattern. The Buddha-like figure would be intended to allay police suspicion and yet, for a Christian, to signify Christ 'the Light of the World' in the guise of 'the Englightened One'. A very similar cross has been discovered and described (in an American newspaper) by Prof. Paul Tagita of the Catholic University of Nagoya, Japan.
Drawing: Helen S. Butler. Courtesy of Professor Arno Lehmann, Halle.

Plate XXXIV, 2

The Gospel Side of the Church of San Juan Bautista, Badoc, Prov. Ilocos Sur, Luzon Is., Philippines. The extreme of 'earthquake baroque'.
Courtesy of Richard E. Ahlborn.

Plate XXXV

The Killing-Stone at Bau, Fiji. Used for the sacrifice of victims to be eaten in pre-Christian war-rites. It has now been made into the font at the Cakobau Memorial Church (Methodist) at Bau.
Courtesy of Rev. Prof. A. R. Tippett, of the Fuller Theological Seminary, Pasadena, Cal., U.S.A.

Plate XXXVI, 1

'The Meal in the House of Simon'. Luke 7:36-50. A mural by school-children at Pompabus, Wabag Valley, Papua New Guinea. They are of the Enga tribe, which was unknown to Europeans till the 20th cent. and not evangelized till 1945. In 1970 the children of

the Roman Catholic Steyler Mission's school at Pompabus created a set of pictures illustrating the whole Bible, with all the persons and scenes shown as completely Papuan;
in the next year the best of these pictures were selected for enlargement onto the walls
of the mission church, by a communal effort, in which the ablest of the children outlined
the scenes and selected the colours and the less gifted applied the paints.

Courtesy of Missio, Aachen.

Plate XXXVI, 2

Ancestral Spirit-Figures, like those prominent in the pre-Christian cults of Papua New
Guinea, used in the pillars of Ngasegalatu Church, 1958. Carver, Dawidi. In this context,
the figures represent not only the tribal ancestors, but also prophets and evangelists,
the spiritual ancestors of Christians.

Courtesy of Professor Arno Lehmann, Halle.

Plate XXXVI, 3

Faces of Ancestors and Scraps of Traditional Design, Papua New Guinea. A page from
one of six note-books written by Moihen, of E. Sapik Prov., New Guinea, a man who
was at the time a leader in a millenarian movement. This cult led to mass hysteria and
visions, resulting in police action in 1956, with the authorities stamping out the cult in
the village and arresting the man. On his release from jail he led a movement of his own,
and was again threatened with arrest. He then withdrew from village life and for two
years lived in seclusion in the forest. There a spirit entered him and stimulated him to
write the six note-books about the history of his people, their ancestors and nature-spirits
(*masalai*). At that time he could read what he had written; by 1976 he could not. Throughout all this he has believed himself to be a loyal Christian. He is now no longer involved
in millenarian activities, saying that he has 'lost the way'. But his experiences seem to
have helped him; he is now an extremely quiet, calm person, and attends his local chapel
daily.

Courtesy of Dr Bryant Allen, University of Papua New Guinea.

Plate XXXVII, 1

The First Chinese Church of Christ, 1054 South King Street, Honolulu, Hawaii. Designed
by Hart Wood, 1929. A piece of successful and appropriate eclecticism.

Courtesy of Archives of Hawaii.

Plate XXXVII, 2

The Soto-Zen Mission, 1708 Nuuanu Avenue, Honolulu, Hawaii. *C.* 1935. Another piece
of successful and appropriate eclecticism—but this time by way of reaction to, instead of
expression of, Christianity.

Courtesy of Archives of Hawaii.

Plate XXXVIII, 1

Part of the Façade of the Church of San Agustin, Arequipa, Peru. 18th-cent.
Photo: Victor Kennett. Courtesy of Mr Kennett.

Plate XXXVIII, 2

'*Santa Prisca*', *from the Retable of the Church of SS. Sebastian and Prisca, Taxco, México.*
1748/58.
Courtesy of Mrs Ann Virginia Owen and the Mexican Embassy, London.

Plate XXXIX, 1

The Church of Parinacota, Chile. 1789. Rustic materials and craftsmanship, but in
complete good taste. The interior is decorated with primitive frescoes.
Courtesy of the Chilean Embassy, London.

Plate XXXIX, 2

Gothic Vaulting in the Church of Yruriria, Guanajuato, México. Mid-16th-cent. A typical
survival of Gothic in vaulting, on Renaissance-type pillars.
Fotografía del Archivo de la Dirección de Monumentos Coloniales, México. Courtesy
of Mrs Ann Virginia Owen and the Mexican Embassy, London.

Plate XL, 1

Mexican Feather-Mosaic: '*The Pantocrator*'. Museo del Virreinto, Tepotzotlán. 16th-cent.
Courtesy of Mrs Ann Virginia Owen and the Mexican Embassy, London.

Plate XL, 2

The '*Ambras Mitre*': *Mexican Featherwork.* Museum für Völkerkunde, Vienna. Back
view: a 'Jesse Tree' showing the Kings of Judah leading to the Virgin and Child. The
front has a similar tree of the Apostles leading to the Crucifixion. A similar mitre in Toledo
was the gift of Vasco de Quiroga, Bishop of Michoacán, to a European potentate. There
are other feather-work mitres at the Escorial, Florence and Singen.
Photo: Fritz Mandl. Courtesy of the Museum für Völkerkunde, Wien.

Plate XLI, 1

St Jude's, Frobisher Bay, N.W.T., Canada: the cathedral of the Anglican Diocese of
the Arctic. 1970/2. Built by Eskimo workmen, with an Eskimo foreman, to a design which
recalls the traditional Eskimo snow-house or *igloo*. Inside, the communion rails have been
made from sleds, and the tapestries woven by Eskimo women, showing Christian scenes
in local modes.
Courtesy of the late Rev. D. Whitbread (recently Archdeacon of the Arctic).

Plate XLI, 2

'*Nuestra Señora del Rosario*': 18th-cent. Mexican work, polychrome with porcelain
eyes, in the Clerics' Chapel at the Santa Barbara Mission, California.
Courtesy of Dr Kurt Baer.

Plate XLI, 3

'*San Rafael*': Oil on canvas, at the Santa Inés Mission, California. Much Indianized,
even to the head-band of an Indian chief.
Photo: Dr Kurt Baer, Santa Barbara College, University of California. Courtesy of
Dr Kurt Baer.

Plate XLII, 1

'*El Santo Niño de Atocha*'. C. 1845/50, by a folk-artist from Old Mexico. Importation of such art, along with popular engravings, into New Mexico was common at the time, and provided the prototypes for the locally-made *santos*. A typical provincial imitation of academic art. On loan from the Cady Wells Collection, to the Spanish Colonial Department, Museum of New Mexico, Santa Fe.

Photo: Dr José E. Espinosa. Courtesy of Cady Wells and the Museum of New Mexico.

Plate XLII, 2

A Miniature Retable, 91½ × 61 cm., for use in a small *oratorio*, painted in tempora over a gesso ground on a pine panel. In the style of José Aragon, a New Mexican artist of Spanish descent and cultural tradition, whose dated works are of 1825/35. The subjects are: Top: St Francis Xavier, Our Lady of Refuge, St John of Nepomuk; Centre, the Holy Family; Bottom: St Antony of Padua, St Rosalia of Palermo, St Antony again. The artist was evidently having difficulty with his arches, which are unknown in the adobe architecture of New Mexico. On loan from the Cady Wells Collection, to the Spanish Colonial Department, Museum of New Mexico.

Photo: Ernest Knee, Santa Fe. Courtesy of Cady Wells and the Museum of New Mexico.

Plate XLIII, 1

'*The Visit of the Magi*'. By H. Speck. The Magi arrive from the East in the only way that could be imagined by a North American Indian.

Courtesy of the United Society for the Propagation of the Gospel, London.

Plate XLIII, 2

André Pierre, Sirène. A *vaudou* picture of a sea-goddess, consort of Agoué, worshipped with feasts and champagne. The artist, once a farmer and now a full-time *vaudou* expert and deacon, lives, despite a growing demand for his pictures, in a modest hut beside a *vaudou* temple on the outskirts of Port-au-Prince, Haiti.

Plate XLIV, 1

A Fetish from Guatemala. Author's Collection. 14 × 9 cm. Composed of two bazaar Christian prints, pinned and stuck together, along with some coloured ribbons and fabric, to form a kind of collage card. The smaller picture appears to be of a Latin American cult-image of the Virgin. The larger is a print of Murillo's masterpiece in the Museo de Bellas Artes, Sevilla, representing the story of the Crucified leaning down to embrace St Bernard, a story which in post-Tridentine times became attached also to St Francis of Assisi. (Murillo's picture closely follows that by Ribalta in the Museo Provincial de Bellas Artes, Valencia.) The whole object was made up, as his fetish, by a Mayan Indian, who was then an animist but under Roman Catholic influence; when later he received (Protestant) baptism he gave it up to the officiating missionaries; by them it was given to Rev. Prof. A. R. Tippett, who was present; he in turn gave it to the author.

Photo: Roger David, Swansea, Wales.

Plate XLIV, 2

A Domestic Model of a Peruvian Cruz del Camino. Author's Collection. $40\frac{1}{2} \times 26 \times 10$ cm. Highly coloured; adorned with the Holy Ghost as a descending dove, a three-dimensional Veronica's veil, the Instruments of the Passion, a St Peter's cock, and a Nativity scene. This is a copy, for a domestic devotional ornament, of the big crosses carried in village processions and set up by the wayside, or carved in stone for the village square.

Photo: Roger David, Swansea, Wales.

Plate XLV

An Earthenware Pietà. Author's Collection. $30\frac{1}{2} \times 17\frac{1}{2} \times 12$ cm. Painted in earth colours. By Tineo of Ayacucho, son of the famous Hilario and Georgina Mendivel of Cuzco, who make figures for sale at the '*Santurantikuy*', the Christmas fair at Cuzco. Mary and the Magdalen are shown as Peruvian peasant women, and their grief is a crushing yet a holy grief.

Photo: Roger David, Swansea, Wales.

Plate XLVI

A Cucumari Pot. Author's Collection. $21\frac{1}{2} \times 15\frac{1}{4} \times 28$ cm. From Quinua, near Ayacucho. The upper part is not unlike the ordinary Christian cross-candlestick; but the lower part is a model of the snouted head of a *cucumari* (one ear is missing in this specimen); this creature is a bogey-animal who was an ancient nature-deity, and who now lends his power to put a spell on any unfortunate whose figure is put on his image. In this case, it would seem that an over-enthusiastic football fan was aiming to cast a spell on the goalkeeper of a rival team!

Photo: Roger David, Swansea, Wales.

Plate XLVII

A Peruvian Domestic Retable. Author's Collection. $16\frac{1}{4} \times 7 \times 32\frac{1}{2}$ cm. The upper shelf shows the raising of a *cruz del camino* (*cf.* Plate XLIV, 2); the lower, a village hat-shop (an important element in the life of a Peruvian village, where the hat indicates the status and provenance of the wearer). Retables such as this are domestic ornaments, now often partly or wholly secularized, but originally imitating the portable retables once carried by missionary priests for use with their altar-stones. The figures are made of a secret compound of gypsum, glue (or honey?) and potato-starch.

Photo: Roger David, Swansea, Wales.

Plate XLVIII

'Christ in Majesty': A Peruvian Folk-Painting. Author's Collection. 32×27 cm. Vegetable colours on gesso on hide. Christ engagingly surrounded by scenes from the rural life of Perú in the artist's time.

Photo: Roger David, Swansea, Wales.

PLATES I-XLVIII

Plate I

2. 'The Nativity', according to the Qu'rān

1. An Early-Seventeenth-Century Christian Fresco from an Aleppo House

Plate II

2. A Christian Miniature by Muḥammad (Paolo) Zamān

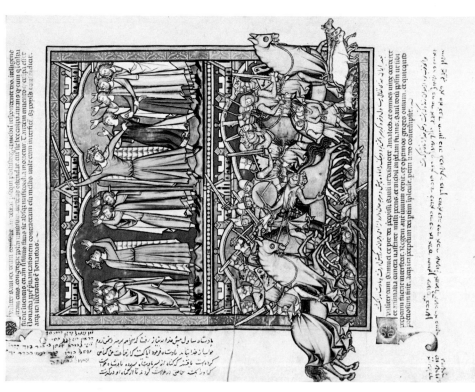

1. A Page from a Book of Old Testament Illustrations presented to Shāh-ʿAbbās I

Plate III

2. The Bethlehem Church, New Julfa

1. The Bethlehem Church, New Julfa

Plate IV

2. 'The Raising of the widow of Cain's Son', modern Persian painting.

1. The Church of St Simon the Zealot, Shīrāz

Plate V

2. The Church of N. S. do Monte, Velha Goa

1. The Basilica of Bom Jesus, Velha Goa

Plate VI

1. The Sanctuary, Great St Thomas' Mount Church, Madras

2. The Church of N. S. da Piedade, Panelim, Goa

Plate VII

1. The Chapel of N. S., Mormugão Fort, Goa

2. The Santadurga Temple, Queulá, Goa

Plate VIII

1. The Church of the Holy Rosary, Tejgaon, Dacca

2. Early-Seventeenth Credence Table from the Jesuits' Church, Lahore

Plate IX

An Eighteenth-Century South Indian 'Crucifixion' on Cotton

Plate X

1. An Early-Eighteenth-Century Goanese Ivory 'Madonna and Child'

2. A Sixteenth-Century Goanese Ivory 'Good Shepherd'

Plate XI

1. The Jesuits Discussing Religion at Akbar's
Court

2. An Early-Seventeenth-Century Mughal Miniature of
'Christ's Entry into Jerusalem'

Plate XII

A Copy of a Contemporary Mughal Miniature of 'Nūr Jahān in her Palace'

Plate XIII

'The Martyrdom of St Cecilia': An Early-Seventeenth-Century Mughal Painting after Wierix

Plate XIV

1. 'The Martyrdom of St Cecilia': A Wierix
Engraving

2. 'The Virgin and Child': An Engraving by Gilles
Sadeler after Mazzola-Bedoli

3. 'The Virgin and Child': A Mughal Painting
after Sadeler

Plate XV

2. 'Adoration of the Virgin and Child': A Mughal Painting

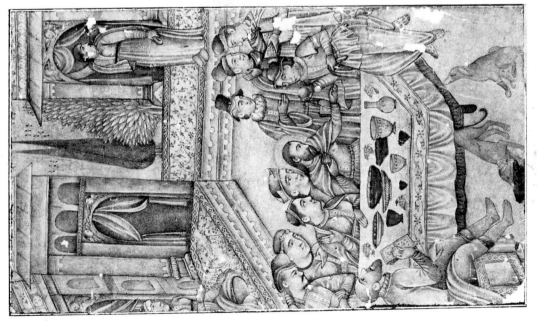

1. 'The Last Supper (?)': A Mughal Drawing

Plate XVI

1. 'S. Paolo fuori le Mura': A Piranesi Engraving

2. 'S. Paolo fuori le Mura': An Indian Painting after Piranesi

Plate XVII

2. The Temple of Viṣṇu, Kālighāt

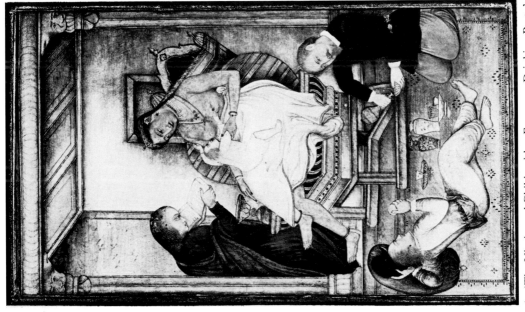

1. 'The Virgin and Child, with a European Drinking Party':
A Mughal Painting

Plate XVIII

1. A Temple Maṇḍapam

2. The Jebalayam (Prayer-room), Tirupattur Āśrama

Plate XIX

2. A Temple Maṇḍapam at Kāñčī XIX, 2

1. West Front of Dornakal Cathedral

Plate XX

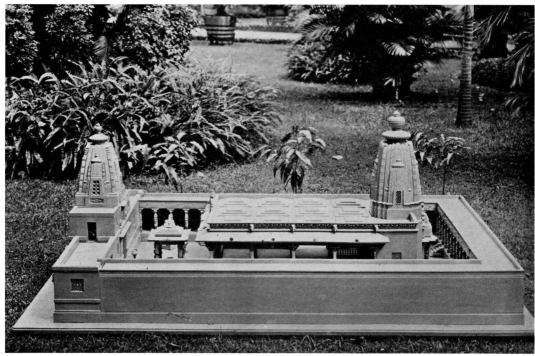

Fr Heras' Maquette for a Church in the South Indian Temple Style

Plate XXI

1. 'The Temptation of Christ', by
A. D. Thomas

2. 'Tamil Christmas', by Sr Genevieve, St. Mary's Convent, Bangalore

Plate XXII

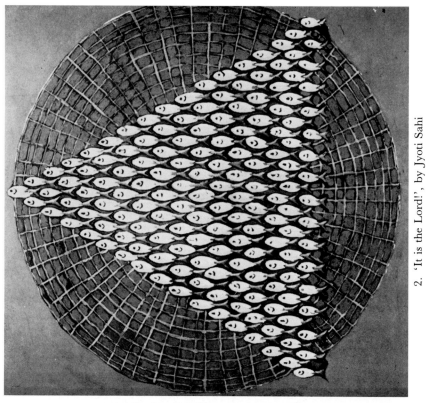

2. 'It is the Lord!', by Jyoti Sahi

1. 'This is Christ the King', by Angelo da Fonseca

Plate XXIII

2. The Indian Secular Christmas!

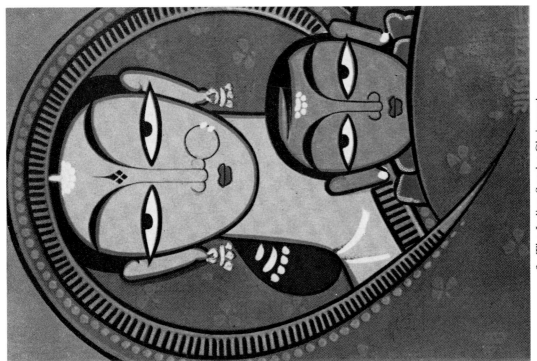

1. 'Tujhe Praṇām', by Jamini Roy

Plate XXIV

From the film 'The Lotus and the Cross': The Crucifixion

Plate XXV

1. A Javanese 'Dives and Lazarus (?)'

2. Phat-Diem Cathedral

Plate XXVI

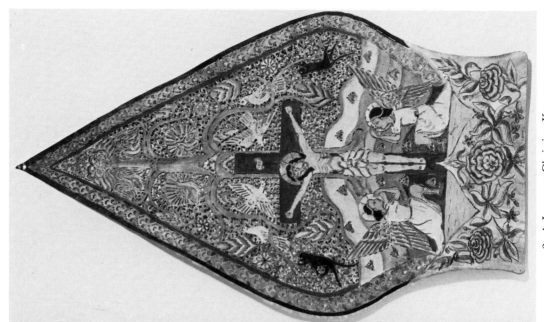

2. A Javanese Christian Kayon

1. A Burmese Crib

Plate XXVII

P. MATTHEVS RICCIVS MACERAT of the Society of Jesus, the first propagator of the Christian Religion in the kingdom of China.

LY PAVLVS GREAT COLAVS OF the Chinese propagator of Christian Law.

2. 'Fr Ricci and Ly Paulus': An Etching by Wencislaus Hollar

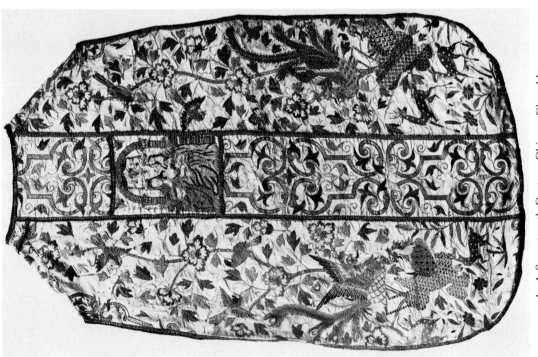

1. A Seventeenth-Century Chinese Chasuble

Plate XXVIII

An Early-Seventeenth-Century Chinese Version of 'Nuestra Señora de l'Antigua'

Plate XXIX

1. 'The Baptism of Christ': An Early-Seventeenth-Century Chinese Plate

2. 'The Crucifixion': An Eighteenth-Century Chinese Plate and Cup

Plate XXX

'Eve Tempting Adam': An Eighteenth-Century Chinese Cup

Plate XXXI

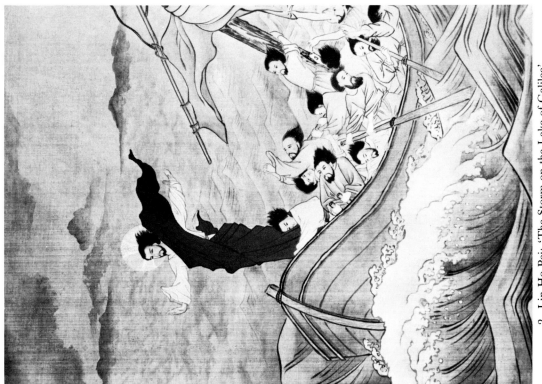

2. Lin Ho Pei: 'The Storm on the Lake of Galilee'

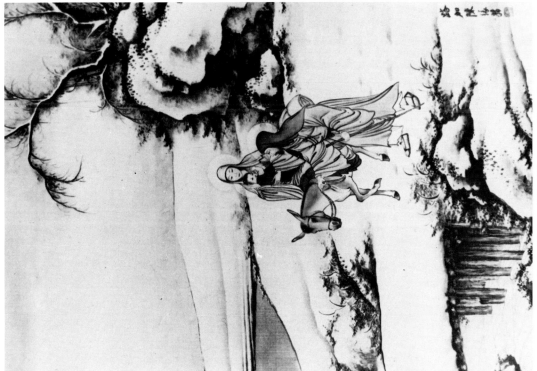

1. Luke Ch'en: 'The Flight into Egypt'

Plate XXXII

2. A Modern Roman Catholic Church in Taiwan

1. 'The Parable of the Importunate Widow': A Modern Chinese Comic Rendering

Plate XXXIII

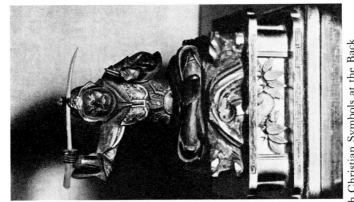

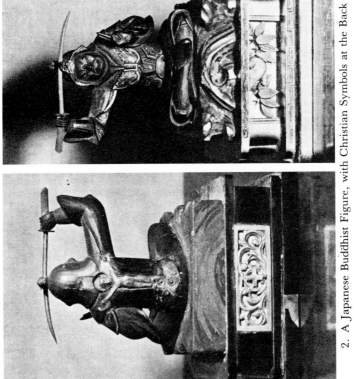

2. A Japanese Buddhist Figure, with Christian Symbols at the Back

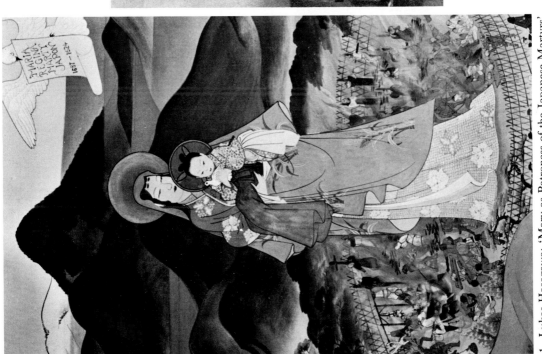

1. Lukas Hasegawa: 'Mary as Patroness of the Japanese Martyrs'

Plate XXXIV

1. A Japanese Cross with a Buddha-Figure

2. The Church of San Juan Bautista, Badoc, Philippines: The Gospel Side

Plate XXXV

The Killing-Stone, Bau, Fiji

Plate XXXVI

1. The Meal in the House of Simon', by School-Children of Pompabus, Papua New Guinea

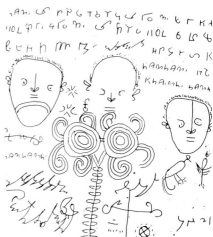

3. Faces of Ancestors and Serafs of Traditional Design, Papua New Guinea

2. Ancestral Spirit-Figures Supporting Nagasepalatu Church,
Papua New Guinea

Plate XXXVII

1. The First Chinese Church of Christ, Honolulu

2. The Soto-Zen Mission, Honolulu

Plate XXXVIII

2. 'Santa Prisca', on the Retable of Taxco Church, México

1. The Church of San Agustín, Arequipa, Peru: Detail of the Façade

Plate XXXIX

2. Yuriria Church, Guanajuato, México: Gothic Vaulting

1. Parinacota Church, Chile

Plate XL

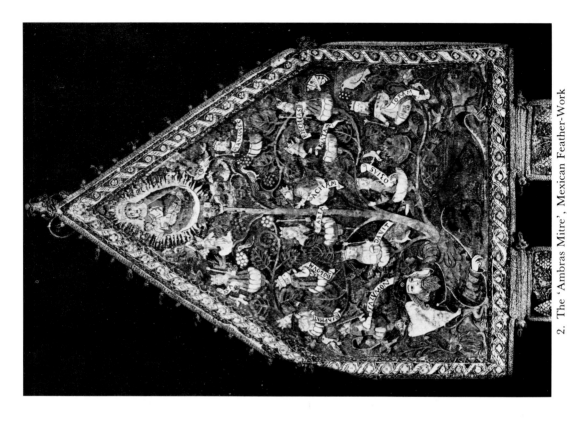

2. The 'Ambras Mitre', Mexican Feather-Work

1. 'The Pantocrator': A Mexican Feather-Mosaic

Plate XLI

1. St Jude's Cathedral, Frobisher Bay, N.W.T., Canada

2. 'Nuestra Señora del Rosario', Santa Barbara, California

3. 'San Rafael', Santa Inès, California

Plate XLII

2. A Miniature Retable, New Mexico

1. 'El Santo Niño de Atocha': A Mexican Folk-Painting

Plate XLIII

1. 'The Visit of the Magi', by H. Speck

2. André Pierre, 'Sirène'

Plate XLIV

2. A Domestic model of a 'Cruz del Camino', Peru

SAN FRANCISC...SIS

TIP. 'SANCHEZ & DE GUISE'

1. A Guatemalan Fetish

Plate XLV

An Earthenware 'Pietà', Peru

Plate XLVI

A Cucumari Pot, Peru

Plate XLVII

A Domestic Retable, Peru

'Christ in Majesty': A Peruvian Folk-Painting